EDUCATIONAL OPPORTUNITY
AND SOCIAL CHANGE
IN ENGLAND

EDUCATIONAL OPPORTUNITY
and Social Change in England

MICHAEL SANDERSON

faber and faber

LONDON · BOSTON

First published in 1987
by Faber and Faber Limited
3 Queen Square London WC1N 3AU

Typeset by Goodfellow & Egan, Cambridge
Printed in Great Britain by
Richard Clay Ltd Bungay Suffolk
All rights reserved

British Library Cataloguing in Publication Data

Sanderson, Michael
Educational opportunity and social change in England.
1. Educational equalization—England—History—20th century
2. Educational equalization—Social aspects—England
I. Title
370.19′0942   I.C213.3.G7

ISBN 0-571-14876-X

HISTORICAL HANDBOOKS

Series Editors:
Avner Offer – University of York
F. M. L. Thompson – Institute of Historical Research,
University of London

It is widely recognized that many of the problems of present-day society are deeply rooted in the past, but the actual lines of historical development are often known only to a few specialists, while the policy-makers and analysts themselves frequently rely on a simplified, dramatized, and misleading version of history. Just as the urban landscape of today was largely built in a world that is no longer familiar, so the policy landscape is shaped by attitudes and institutions formed under very different conditions in the past. This series of specially commissioned handbooks aims to provide short, up-to-date studies in the evolution of current problems, not in the form of narratives but as critical accounts of the ways in which the present is formed by the past, and of the roots of present discontents. Designed for those with little time for extensive reading in the specialized literature, the books contain full bibliographies for further study. The authors aim to be as accurate and comprehensive as possible, but not anodyne; their arguments, forcefully expressed, make the historical experience available in challenging form, but do not presume to offer ready-made solutions.

CONTENTS

TABLES

PREFACE

In the course of human history mankind has been wasteful of nothing so much as of its own ability. What undeveloped genius there may have been among the nomadic tribes of North America or Central Asia in past centuries we can never know. Whether some Anglo-Saxon minstrel had the potential of a Mozart, or some Norman mason the aptitudes of a Newton is lost to us. The medieval Church was a powerful mechanism for catching the abilities of those of modest or lowly origins and providing a career open to talent for a Becket (a merchant's son) or a Wolsey (a butcher's son) and in Tudor times ambitious humanists and lawyers used Oxford and Cambridge as stepping stones to positions of power and influence. In the last two centuries or so there have been quite exceptional men who have been able to rise academically even through a very defective educational system. William Whewell, the son of a Lancaster carpenter, clambered up from Lancaster Charity School to Heversham Grammar School, to Cambridge and Mastership of Trinity in 1842. His near contemporary Isaac Milner, 1750–1820, the President of Queens', was likewise a former weaver.

Yet, notwithstanding such exceptional cases, it is only in very recent times that it has been regarded in England as desirable and even an obligation of state to organize such a flow of talent through the educational system. It has been done partly out of a sense of self-interest to increase social efficiency and national wealth and partly out of a democratic concern for the rights to self-fulfilment of the individual. Economists came to appreciate this. Alfred Marshall, calling for more middle-grade schools and scholarships, observed in 1890 that

There is no greater extravagance more prejudicial to the growth of the national wealth than that wasteful negligence which allows genius that happens to be born of lowly parentage to expend itself in lowly work.[1]

and a generation later P. H. Wicksteed made explicit the connection of this with educational opportunity:

> those occupations which require an elaborate and expansive preparation will, so long as present conditions remain, always be recruited from a small section of society; and the talent which exists in the great mass of the people will be either undetected or left untrained.

Accordingly the educational system should be

> a great sorting machine for adjusting the opportunities to capacities throughout the whole population.[2]

An array of mechanisms came to be employed in this adjustment of 'capacities' to 'opportunities'. Elementary education became obligatory for all and its age range increased, 'secondary' education was divided off as a separate stage and differentiated into types according to intelligence. The whole structure was laced together with examinations to select and motivate, while scholarships rewarded success and prevented academic progress from being impeded by the limitations of the social and financial background of the candidate. Such arrangements became common in advanced countries, and in England came into being from around 1900.

An examination of this increasing educational opportunity in England since 1900 is the subject of this book. Its span begins in the late-Victorian period when it was accepted that elementary and secondary education were for quite different social classes and less than one per cent of the population went to university. It finishes in the present day with universal secondary education and the immensely widened post-secondary facilities of the 1980s. It is not, of course, a total history of education of these years, but approaches the subject from this particular point of view – the widening access to education and the flow of ability through the changing structures of the system.

There is good reason for doing this. Most general histories of education necessarily cover a range of themes which precludes focusing on this specific aspect. Professor Harold Silver's *Equal Opportunity in Education* is an interesting exception although it is more in the nature of a collection of document extracts than a thematic or statistical analysis. The potential original literature is immense since there is a first-rate tradition of investigation in this field from the work of R. H. Tawney and Kenneth Lindsay in the 1920s through to the classics of J. W. B. Douglas, A. H. Halsey and others in post-war and recent years. The vastness and variety of the literature poses problems for the student and the general reader since it exceeds what could be studied even on a specialist course. Yet such is the importance of the topic that both specialist student and general reader need the main themes and findings within a manageable compass. It is hoped that this synthesis will serve this purpose.

We hope, also, to overcome the problem of fusing the past and the present. Social history since the Edwardians merges into socio-logical surveys and in turn into reflections on the contemporary scene and speculation about the future. The present necessarily grows out of the past. Accordingly an evolutionary view of the present is necessary to explain both the rationale of contemporary arrangements and to evaluate the progress made during this century – the first consciously to plan for widening access to education at all levels.

Chapter I considers some problems of educational opportunity in the mid/late 1980s. Chapters II and III will look back to the evolution of policy and the resulting changes in access from the reforms of the 1900s to the Butler Act of 1944, and thence to the present. Since there is an inevitable interconnection between changing policies, structures and ideology, Chapter IV looks at the concepts behind the system. These range from the Edwardian images of 'ladders' of opportunity, through debates about the meaning of equality, to modern notions of pools of ability and stocks of human capital. Chapter V sets the changing access to education in a wider social context of factors influencing the supply and demand for its facilities. These include political attitudes to state education, the levels of public finance for the service, and the perception of consumers about the relation of education to occupational change, earnings and social mobility. Since England's experience is shared with many other advanced countries Chapter VI examines England's performance in comparison with her leading rivals to highlight the common factors and our unusual deficiencies – notably in the post-school education of non-academic teenagers.

I

The Contemporary Crisis

Infants and comprehensive standards

That education at the present time faces many critical problems is all too evident. This is highlighted by the replacing of Sir Keith Joseph by Mr Kenneth Baker as Secretary of State for Education and the re-emergence of education high on the political agenda. In this introductory chapter we want to review the contemporary state of access to education at various levels of the system before we examine the historical evolution of policies, structures and concepts which have shaped educational opportunity in this century.

The initial non-compulsory area of education where the discretion of parents determines access is the pre-school education of the under-fives. The value of this is now well appreciated. American experience with the Headstart pre-schooling scheme has indicated that children who have experienced such programmes read better, are less likely to fail in primary school, stay at school longer and are less likely to be unemployed or to be arrested in adult life. The English position is not bad – though with ample scope for improvement. Of 16,000 children born in one week in 1970 more than half were in school by the age of 4½.[1] In the 1980s some 42 per cent of 3- and 4-year-olds are receiving nursery education,[2] but beyond that, many more children are experiencing some form of pre-schooling in play groups. This is not, however, quite as good as the situation in France and Belgium, which have virtually complete school education for 3- and 4-year-olds or Germany with three-quarters so provided.

The moving down of the normal school starting age from 5 to 4 may come about in England as a result of the falling birth rate. As LEAs find that they have excess capacity due to declining numbers of 11- to 16–year-olds so some are considering using the space and resources for younger age groups including 4–year-olds. This is so in Leeds, for example, which is planning 4–11 primary schools which may become a 'national trend setter'.[3]

One crucial factor affecting the flow of talent in recent years has been the comprehensive reorganization since the 1960s: has it stimulated or baulked that flow by raising or lowering academic standards? If the new comprehensives had led to a decline in taking and passing examinations which provided access to further stages of education then they could be accused of impeding the potential flow of talent. If, on the contrary, there has been an increase then they could be seen as a more effective talent pump than the system they replaced.

At the factual statistical level standards have undoubtedly risen over the last 20 years of comprehensivization.[4]

Table 1: *Proportions of children passing GCE and CSE examinations*

Percentage of	1964/5	1984/5
English school leavers obtaining		
1 or more A level pass	12.9	17.1
5 or more GCE O level or CSE Grade 1	20.3	26.9
1 or more GCE O level or CSE Grade 1	36.0	54.7
No graded examination pass	64.0	9.4

Leading analysts A. H. Halsey and Anthony Heath of Oxford and Stuart Maclure, former editor of the *Times Educational Supplement*, concur that there has undoubtedly been an increase of qualified schoolchildren, no perceptible decline of standards, if not much equality either.[5]

Yet the collateral question is not only whether comprehensivization has been accompanied by an increase in standards but whether comprehensives perform better than the alternatives. Marks and Pomian-Srzednicki in 1985[6] found that pupils in the remaining secondary modern and grammar schools obtained between 30 and 40 per cent more O level passes per pupil than those in comprehensive schools. Best of all were independent schools in the Assisted Places Scheme. The problem with such a study is that it is difficult to standardize for social class. Is it fair to compare working class children in comprehensives with upper middle class ones in grammar schools? Ideally one would wish to compare the same social class in different selective and non-selective schools. The other problem is that there are now so few children in the selective system: 31,000 in secondary moderns and 17,000 in grammar schools out of a total of 380,000 in the survey by Marks and Pomian-Srzednicki. Standards vary massively between different comprehensives themselves, more than between comprehensives as a group and other schools. No doubt some comprehensives (like some private schools) do not 'stretch' some pupils sufficiently academically and many have to cope with appallingly adverse social environments. But these problems would also have faced late developers consigned as failures to the secondary modern schools under the selective system. One is left with imponderables. Would grammar school successes in the 1940s and 1950s have done as well in the comprehensives of the 1970s and 1980s? Would some comprehensive successes of the 1980s have done as well if they had been allocated to modern schools in the 1950s? We cannot possibly know what this balance of loss and gain might be. Yet the expanding examination figures cited earlier do suggest that, overall, the comprehensives have acted as a pump stimulating access upwards rather than a baulk against it.

Vocational technology for teenagers

For all the attention paid to it, comprehensivization may affect the flow of ability less than the questionable state of the education we offer mid-teenagers. Here there is an urgent need for reform to raise the scientific and vocational content and orient it towards industry and the world of work. Herein lies a complex of troubles and responses.

The basic difficulty is the low wages and status of school teachers, especially in the sciences, craft and technology, which have been deteriorating to a nadir in recent years. As easy victims of policies of public pay restraint and the cutting of public expenditure, they have seen private pay settlements move sharply ahead of their own and of inflation. In these circumstances many science and other teachers have quitted their thankless task. Meanwhile, at this time of good graduate employment (1986) young graduates are shunning teaching, and especially science teaching, in droves.

The present situation is very dangerous. The poor state of teachers is well known. Between 1975 and 1985 prices rose by 240 per cent, average earnings by 287 per cent and average salaries by 292 per cent. Teachers' salaries lagged behind all these, rising by only 219 per cent.[7] In particular they have suffered a sharp decline in real wages from 1980,[8] circumstances which underlaid their 1985–6 strike. Some 7,500 teachers left the profession in 1985–6[9] and the ILEA was left with 70 unfilled headships at the beginning of 1986.[10] In midsummer 1986 there were nationally 380 unfilled posts in mathematics and 180 in physics.[11] Graduates choosing teaching as a career fell by 11.5 per cent in 1984–5[12] and a further 19 per cent in 1985–6. Graduates proposing to teach mathematics have fallen by 16 per cent, physics by 11 per cent and chemistry by 25 per cent.[13] No Cambridge physics graduate at all went into teaching in 1985.[14] The knock-on effects over many years have been dire. The HMI's 1986 report found that 30 per cent of lessons were badly taught by inadequate teachers and that many teachers were teaching subjects in which they had no qualifications, chiefly in science.[15] Indeed over a quarter of those teaching mathematics and a third of those teaching physics were unqualified to do so. In a market economy the consumer gets what he pays for and in a context in which the taxpayer has been unwilling – or politically not allowed – to let his taxes flow into teachers' salaries the result has been deplorable but scarcely surprising. As a comprehensive deputy head observed, teachers 'have been underpaid for so long that the quality of the staff is poor'.[16] This is not only unfortunate for teachers and children, it is deeply worrying for parents, employers, industry and the country at large.

In spite of the very high levels of general unemployment industry is experiencing a stifling shortage of people with mathematics and physics based skills for electronics, engineering, computing and so forth. This is so from school leavers to graduate levels. Because of the poor pay able mathematicians and physicists no longer teach. Accordingly too many mediocre or unqualified teachers try to cope with these subjects and this is proving inadequate to motivate sufficient of their pupils to continue with science or to win high grades. Indeed only a third of 16-year-olds who take the examination pass mathematics at O level or CSE Grade 1.[17] In turn too few well-prepared teenagers pass on to further and higher education in the hard sciences. Since they are relatively scarce their incomes in industry soar, diminishing any likelihood of their returning to teaching. The vicious circle continues for not only is education the loser but the firms themselves. GEC and Plessey constantly complain of the shortage of skilled labour, the latter experiencing a 12.5 per cent gap between the supply and demand of graduate engineers.[18] Overall 10 per cent of CBI firms reported that shortage of skilled labour was handicapping their expansion.[19]

The poverty and paucity of science and mathematics teaching also makes a nonsense of other pieces of otherwise good Government policy. For example in 1985 it was announced that £143m would be made available to provide 4,000 extra student places in engineering and technology.[20] Yet this overlooked the fact that there were *already* 1,100 *unfilled* places in universities in science and technology (including 408 in engineering and computing).[21] Schools were simply not producing sufficient qualified applicants worth accepting by university science departments at *any* low A level grade. The idea that creating another 4,000 places would in turn conjure into existence suitable applicants to fill them in a decade of demographic contraction is fantasy. Another scheme announced within a few days of the former was that all pupils should be taught science for the whole of their school lives, from 5 to 16. This was to be with due emphasis on 'intellectual demands' and 'rigour', and was to include the whole gamut of 'scientific concepts, skills and processes, technological applications and social consequences'![22] Both these policies are totally admirable, they are the kinds of measures the Germans and Japanese have the wealth and the will to afford. But in the present state of the underpaid, undervalued weakness of English school science teaching they smack of policy-making by wishful thinking gimmickry rather than a serious address to the root of the problem.

Various measures are being mooted or put into action to try to break this bottleneck of the flow of young people into technology-based vocational training. Some major firms are trying to ease the situation. GEC provides consultancy jobs for schools mathematics teachers during the vacations to top up their salaries. ICI channels ex-employees into science teaching and has provided some 250 in this way.[23]

Government initiatives in various directions are seeking to raise the level of science and technology in schools and beyond. The General Certificate of Secondary Education (GCSE) began in September 1986 to replace O level and CSE. Whereas the previous examination system left too many pupils with no qualifications at all at O level, the new examination is intended to provide some 80 per cent with a qualification. Moreover it will emphasize laboratory experiments, practical skills in craft design and technology and applied mathematics.[24] The initially absurd underfunding has been improved somewhat and the emphasis on practical vocationalism is a step in the right direction.

The Technical and Vocational Education Initiative is also welcomed as a move in the direction of a more Germanic approach to vocational education. This began in 1983 as a pilot scheme by the Manpower Services Commission and by 1986 was operating in 73 LEAs. The idea is that schools devise courses with direct business and technological application, working with computers and word processors, studying such fields as practical craft and graphic design, building and construction. Pupils opt and are selected to take such courses, and schools mounting them for 14- to 18-year-olds are given more funds. In 1986 some 50,000 pupils have been on courses and their success has prompted the expansion of the scheme nationwide with £90m to be spent over the next 10 years.[25]

Most important for school leavers has been the Youth Training Scheme run by the Manpower Services Commission. About a third of school leavers go into it and about £1bn a year is spent on it (the Germans spend £6bn on apprentice training). It is designed to counteract the decline in apprenticeships in engineering firms, for example, from 25,000 a year in the 1970s to between 6,000 and 7,000 a year by the mid-1980s. The decline has naturally come about because so many of the engineering firms which provided them have gone out of business. The YTS initially offered a year of training to all 16-year-olds who might otherwise be unemployed. Some 100,000 employers take part and young people receive training and work experience rather than remaining idle. Sixty per cent of the 389,000 boys and girls who joined YTS in 1984–5 gained permanent employment and a further six per cent went on to further training.[26] The scheme is throwing off the stigma of merely providing 'free boys' as almost Victorian workhouse sweated labour and in 1986 YTS has been extended to a two-year scheme.

From September 1987 all these measures will be supplemented by the College of the Air. In this scheme radio and television programmes on technological and commercial subjects will be transmitted overnight. These courses will not provide qualifications but supplement studies towards those of the City and Guilds, RSA and other institutions.

Most recent and especially to be welcomed is the plan for City Technical Colleges announced by Mr Kenneth Baker at the Conservative Party Conference of 1986. Some 20 large CTCs will be established from 1988 to take children aged 11 to 18 and give them a curriculum strongly directed to science, technology, business and work experience. Independent of the LEAs, they will be funded directly by the DES with contributions from industry towards their capital cost. Teachers of quality are expected to be attracted by high salaries though this has aroused fears that this will divert resources and talent from the already starved LEA maintained sector.[27]

All these measures are imaginative attempts to provide a bridge of access between school and vocational training and the world of work. Yet for the historian there looms behind all these modern devices – GCSE, TVEI, YTS, CTC – the ghost of the Edwardian junior technical school. We shall argue later that the failure to develop this form of school in the inter-war years and in the implementation of the 1944 Act is probably the worst single defect of English education in the twentieth century and a major cause of our present problems. Although we cannot turn the clock back to recreate this form as an alternative for non-academic teenagers, some of its characteristics are being resurrected by these new schemes. This is especially so with the CTCs though their in-evitably modest number cannot substitute for the lack of a national system. None the less they are a desirable development.

But behind all this lies the lesson of the last few years. There is no point in purporting to devise policies to increase the science and technology bias in education and its vocational links with industry while allowing science teachers's salaries to become so totally uncompetitive. The undermanned, under-resourced and under-qualified state of much science – and conspicuously mathematics –

teaching is a rotten weakness in the link between education and industry. The policies that have brought this situation about have been contrary to the best interests of the nation.

The independent sector

The public, or independent schools, as they have preferred to call themselves since 1985, have been major beneficiaries in changes in the flow of young people through the education system. The replacing of grammar schools by comprehensives in the 1960s and 1970s and especially the abolition of the direct grant grammar schools in 1975 prompted many middle class parents to think of public schools as an alternative. The deterioration of the state sector in the 1980s and the disruption caused by the teachers' pay and service dispute 1985–6 impelled yet more parents from the state to the private sector.

In spite of a 3.7 per cent fall in the number of pupils in state secondary schools those in independent schools rose by 1.1 per cent between 1985 and 1986.[28]

Table 2: Boys and girls at independent schools, 1984–5, 1985–6

	1984–5	1985–6	
Day boys at independent schools	138,569	142,567	+2.9%
Day girls at independent schools	166,061	167,909	+1.1%
Boarding boys at independent schools	72,654	70,977	−2.3%

The Assisted Places Scheme also encouraged the shift from state to independent sector. Between 1981, when the scheme started, and 1985, 17,386 assisted places were taken up out of an available total of 20,702, at a cost of £22.5m to the taxpayer.[29] Of those benefiting from the scheme about 40 per cent receive free places. That not all places have yet been taken up is attributed to the fact that the ceiling of £16,000 parental income is regarded as too low and that a slight raising of this scarcely affluent upper limit would bring in more families of modest means who would wish to benefit. It was hoped that by 1990 as many as one in seven, and in some schools up to a third, of pupils would be bright children from low income families under the scheme.[30]

The independent schools have a firm position within the present structure. They are highly resourced (spending over £100m on new and improved buildings and equipment in 1985) and their high standards provide an exemplar for the state sector. Although educating only six per cent of all school children they provide a quarter of all university students.[31] Their abolition is improbable for two practical reasons apart from the theoretical considerations of Chapter IV. Firstly the bulk of opinion is against abolition. A MORI poll of 1982 found 76 per cent opposed to the abolition of the public schools, while one for Gabbitas Thring in 1985 found only 20 per cent in favour.[32] Secondly the costs of abolition or absorption are impracticable as two estimates suggest:

Table 3: Estimates of the savings to the state sector of independent schools

	Schools	School places	Capital costs necessary to absorb into the state sector	Annual salary savings
Lord Hailsham[33]		310,000		£310m
John Izbicki[34]	2400		£2bn	£500m

Preoccupation persists in some quarters with the narrow social range of the public schools and their capacity to transmit privilege across the generations. In the most recent analysis Irene Fox found the following spread of occupations among the parents of public schoolboys:[35]

Table 4: Occupations of fathers of public schoolboys, 1985

Administrators and officials	25.9%
Self employed professionals	18.4%
Large and small proprietors	16.4%
Industrial managers	8.9%
Farmers	10.0%

A single lorry driver made up the working-class element. This is hardly surprising, but more interesting are her findings on the grandparents of public schoolboys. It was evident that nearly half (46 per cent) of men in Social Class I (senior administrators, professional men, industrial managers, large proprietors) who sent their children to public schools had fathers who were already in Social Class I themselves. Grandfathers' status was maintained by their sons who in turn were hoping to transmit it across three generations by sending their own children to public schools.

It is considerations of this nature, in spite of the high costs of abolition referred to earlier, that have prompted the Labour Party to indicate that it would phase out fee paying schools by with-drawing all subsidies and concessions.[36] It would abolish the Assisted Places Scheme, abolish charitable status, impose VAT on fees and eventually eradicate the schools altogether. Forewarned, the schools have created a committee to co-ordinate a campaign in their defence.[37] Access to the independent schools remains a problem though a more likely approach to it is to widen that access rather than abolish it altogether.

The ethnic minority problem

One very distinctive issue in the flow of ability in the education system is that of ethnic minorities comprising some 2.5 million persons. Increasing anxiety in the late 1960s and 1970s about the poor performance of West Indians in particular led to the setting up of the inquiry in 1979 which reported under Lord Swann in 1985. The low achievement of West Indians compared with Asians and other ethnic minority children was evident.[38]

Various reasons are advanced for this disparity. The view that West Indians have some inherent genetic intellectual inferiority was dismissed by Swann. A study for the Swann Report by Professor Nicholas Macintosh of Cambridge concluded that West Indians' low IQ more likely reflected their social disadvantages in income,

Table 5: Percentages of children of ethnic minority groups achieving O, CSE,
A levels and university entrance

%	West Indians		Asians		Other Leavers	
	1978–9	1981–2	1978–9	1981–2	1978–9	1981–2
5 or more O level passes (grades A–C) or CSE Grade 1 passes	3	6	18	17	16	19
1 or more A level passes	2	5	13	13	12	13
University entrance	1	1	3	4	3	4

family size and over-crowding.[39] They share the drawbacks
common to the working classes irrespective of race. They lack pre-
school provision and there is a 'gulf in trust' between West Indian
families and schools. Most particularly West Indian children have
undoubtedly encountered racist attitudes among teachers which has
stunted their educational development. This might be hostile –
jokes by teachers about sending black children 'back to the chocolate
factory' – or perversely compassionate.[40] These latter teachers
sentimentally under-estimate the ability of black children, inculcate
low expectations and hold them back from competitive examinations
as a cruel kindness. Yet paradoxically, as the above figures indicate,
West Indian children having taken A levels do use these qualifications to move into higher education much more than expected.
This arises from blacks' belief that their employment prospects are
far worse than for whites of comparable age and ability and that
they more urgently need the enhancement of higher qualifications.

One important scheme to improve the situation is 'special access'
courses started in 1978 to prepare mature adults from the ethnic
minorities without normal entrance qualifications to enter higher
education to train as teachers. Between 1978 and 1984 some 1,800
students have passed through 33 colleges in the scheme. Of these 51
per cent were West Indians.[41] In this pump-priming exercise it is
hoped that providing special access for the few will eventually
improve the general access to higher education for more of the
ability which may be tapped from the ethnic minorities.

Higher education

The problems surrounding access to higher education – comprising 46 universities, 29 polytechnics and 73 colleges of higher education – are among the most serious of the present time. The basic issue is well appreciated. Because of the falling birth rate of the 1960s and 1970s due to the practice of oral contraception the 18- and 19-year-old population is expected to fall by 33 per cent between 1984 and 1996. However, due to an expected sustained or increased demand for university entrance from women, mature and overseas students, the decline in students may not be so drastic but will still be about 14 per cent. The government envisages a fall in student numbers as follows:[42]

Table 6: Estimates of the fall in students in higher education 1983–4 to 1996–7

	Actual	Optimal Variant	Minimal Variant
1983–4	565,000		
1989–90		612,000	566,000
1996–7		525,000	492,000

The Association of University Teachers and the Royal Statistical Society on the contrary believe in the need for a steady expansion of university places until the end of the century.

The contraction in student numbers is also tied in with two other policies, the cutting back of finance and the switch from arts to the sciences. In 1984–5 financial support for the universities amounted to £3.4bn. Although this is modest compared with the big spenders like social security, defence and the health service at £32bn, £15bn and £11bn apiece in 1983–4, it is sizeable and to be reduced. Universities have lost ten per cent of their funding between 1981–6 and will lose another ten per cent over the next five years.

Accordingly, with the university system being contracted before the sharp demographic fall, access to university is becoming more difficult and competitive, with universities 'turning away a distressing number of high quality applicants'.[43] Admissions to universities have fallen slightly in 1979–83 while much of the overspill has been taken up by the polytechnics and other public sector colleges whose admissions have increased by about 30 per cent.

In the latest switch in government policy (1 April 1987) it is now intended to increase full- and part-time students in all forms of higher education from 906,000 in 1986–7 to 957,000 by 1990–1, though with a contraction thereafter down to 1996, when the population of 18-year-olds reaches its lowest point. However, no extra money will be provided to fund this increase.

Another aspect of finance which will affect access to higher education is the level of the student grant. Scarcely had the expansion of the universities begun in the 1960s than the student grant began to fall in real terms and in comparision with alternative earnings.[44] In the present situation the real value of the student grant has fallen by 17 per cent between 1979–80 and 1985–6. The grant of 1986–7 was set in December 1985 to rise by only 2 per cent when the rate of inflation was 5.5 per cent[45] (inflation since sank to 2.4 per cent in the summer of 1986). The disparity prompted the resignation on 17 December 1985 of Mr Robert Rhodes James, the Government's higher education liaison officer over the 'intolerable squeeze' on university finance.[46] In addition to this students lost their entitlement to housing benefit and to unemployment and supplementary benefit. It was clearly unsatisfactory that the student grant system should have become so meshed in with a welfare system designed for totally different people. However it is fair to note that Britain devotes a larger share of national income to higher education and caters for fewer students at higher cost than most of its European neighbours.[47] This results in the high standards and low failure rates associated with the British system. But it does raise the complaint that resources are concentrated on a small proportion of the population at the expense of other post-secondary opportunities. It may be that some form of loan and pay back system may ultimately be devised to reduce the £700m student maintenance bill.

Our concern here is not with the rights and wrongs of this but with the implications of the highly unattractive state of student grants and their potentially deterrent effect for middle-class families – those with, say, residual incomes of £12,000 to £15,000 p.a. The student grant in 1986–7 is £1,870, some 20 per cent less than its 1979–80 value. There has actually been a small fall in the proportion of university students coming from professional families from 23.9 per cent in 1982 to 22.1 per cent in 1984.[48] In so far as it becomes more attractive for able school leavers to join banks, supermarkets and insurance companies etc. rather than undertake the labour and expense of doing a degree in engineering, chemistry, computing etc. this may not be desirable. It will emphasize the preference for service industries over manufacturing and technology which England is rightly seeking to correct. A likely resolution may well be differential grants and generous student salaries paid by scientific manufacturing companies to pre-empt the existing drain on the graduate labour they need and whose lack is causing them anxiety.

Another problem in the flow of ability to and through the universities is that of accommodating both contraction and a further shift towards science and technology. In the 1960s it was believed that the expansion of higher education had led to an undesirable skewing of studies against science and technology and towards the arts. It was true that many of the new universities of the 1960s on their green field sites in cathedral cities projected an image neither very industrial nor technological. There were obvious temptations. To avoid the slow growth of Hull and Keele, for example, many new universities determined on tactical rapid expansion. The low cost arts and social studies were the cheapest way of doing this and the bulge of A level applicants in these subjects fuelled the growth. Polytechnics and technological universities also played their own game, including arts subjects in their curricula as a move towards true university status. For example, there is one city with an excellent university and a polytechnic *both* of which have departments of education, of art history and of music. Rather oddly one of the largest departments of philosophy in Britain is in a polytechnic. The unwillingness in Britain to accept the idea of almost purely scientific and technological institutions of higher education is an old and peculiar tradition and a questionable legacy of Victorian liberal education. It is in sharp and conscious contrast with German attitudes and the concept of the Technical High School and of no evident advantage to us at all. It underlies the contemporary paradox of universities being enjoined to become more like polytechnics while polytechnics strive to become more like universities.

The notion that there is an imbalance in curricula too much tilted towards the arts is a myth as we shall see when we compare England with European countries (p. 134). None the less it is believed that a shift away from the arts is desirable and this is taking place.[49]

Table 7: Percentages of university students in different subject areas

	1979–80	1983–4
Engineering and Science	34.71	37.3
Arts and Social Studies	32.83	31.34

The other subjects were Education, Medicine, Agriculture, Professional and Vocational Subjects, Languages. Collectively their proportion changed scarcely at all from 31.7 per cent in 1979–80 to 30.9 per cent in 1983–4.

This shift is desirable because of the higher employment prospects of many scientists reflecting their economic value. Of first degree graduates of 1983 the following percentages were unemployed at December of that year.[50]

Table 8: Percentages of graduates unemployed, by subject, 1983

Electrical Engineering	6	Sociology	36
General Engineering	9	General Arts	36
Mathematics	12	English	40

Yet it is worth noting from the same source that students of economics (21%), law (21%), accountancy (5%) were less subject to unemployment than chemists (29%) and physicists (23%), whereas the least employable of all were not arts students but geologists (47%) and zoologists (48%). Desirable as it may be to increase the proportion of technology students to those of the pure humanities, it is not self evident from the employment scene that it is beneficial to increase pure scientists at the expense of those economic/social subjects which may be especially relevant to business.

Yet given that a further continued shift is necessary there are certain problems in adjusting the flow in a time of demographic and financial contraction. Firstly, it is not enough simply to increase the number of science places in higher education if there are not the students to fill them. We have already noted the unreality of plans to expand science places by 4,000 at a time when 1,100 remain unfilled. The root problem remains the inadequate flow from the schools which in turn relates to the low state and pay of school science teaching.

Secondly the shift from arts to science entails one from low to high cost. It costs £12,000 to produce a social studies graduate and £13,000 for an arts graduate, compared with £22,500 for an engineer and £24,000 for a physicist.[51] Since there is actually more demand by employers for economists than for physicists costing society twice as much, this should give us pause – especially since physicists and engineers are often wastefully used in general administration in tasks as well done by arts graduates and not requiring scientific skills.[52] To shift from low to high cost subjects while sustaining overall cuts presents the universities with difficult problems which inevitably impede the shift itself.

A third problem in this area is the difficulty of producing more scientists in the context of a fall in overall student numbers into the 1990s. There will be fewer 18-year-olds, yet industry's demand for graduates in those years is not going to fall. Industrial growth is attendant on a wide range of factors within which temporary blips in the number of 18-year-olds is of negligible account. Adjusting university places to falling student numbers and not to the increasing needs of industry does run counter to other laudable objectives of making the universities relevant to industry. Even now, before the contraction in numbers really begins to bite, employment prospects for graduates are strong to the extent that recruitment has become competitive between employers for the first time for some years.[53] If the economic policies of recent years do indeed lead to the desired economic recovery, this competition can only get worse. More contraction in the universities leading to more competition between firms to recruit graduates reflects itself in the high inflationary private sector pay settlements that have become a feature of 1985–6.

This in turn relates to the fourth problem in the 'shift', that of the quality of science teaching in higher education itself. Following the 11 per cent cut of 1981 the Government wanted 3,000 university teachers to take early retirement. In fact 6,300 retired early and a further 5,300 left through natural wastage. But proportionally far more were lost in the sciences and technologies, the very reverse of what was intended.[54] Yet in spite of 'new blood' posts to replace the retired, the level of university salaries is too low to attract and retain replacements of calibre.

Further, it has been Government policy to diminish the numbers of students in universities but to achieve an overall expansion of numbers in higher education by increasing numbers in the polytechnics.[55]

Table 9: Numbers of students in universities and polytechnics 1980–1/1983–4

Students	1980–1	1983–4
Universities	273,000	268,000
Polytechnics	208,000	266,000

The latter, less well resourced, are cheaper, the annual recurrent costs per polytechnic student being £3,125 compared with £4,540 for university students (1982–3). Universities' fears that cuts would lead them to turn away 9,400 students have been removed by an extra grant of £54m in August 1986. This is to be welcomed. Yet it does not disguise the fact that the overall policy is to channel students away from relatively well-resourced universities with often highly qualified staff to polytechnics somewhat less well endowed.

If the immediate outlook for higher education into the 1990s is one of contraction, the prospect beyond is more expansive. A rapid rise in the birthrate is forecast for the early 1990s and the 1986 primary school population of 3.7m is expected to rise to 4.2m by 1998.[57] As this future rolling tide successively buoys up primary, secondary and higher education it will provide a more generous leeway for rethinking the system than the present contraction.

With these considerations on the present let us turn back to see how the developments of the recent past have led us to our contemporary position with all its problems and dilemmas.

II

Policy and Progress from Morant to Butler 1900–1944

The emergence of secondary education

In the mid-nineteenth century the division between elementary and secondary education was one of social class. There was no assumption that children should proceed, with advancing age, from one level to another. Rather, elementary education was seen as that for the 'lower orders', the 'labouring classes', 'the poor' or 'the people' and before 1870 it was largely provided by religious and charitable bodies with some government aid. In R. H. Tawney's words elementary education 'was a self sufficient kind of education designed for a particular section of the community'.[1] Secondary education in the grammar schools and public schools was for a fee paying middle class. Elementary education gave the elements of reading, writing and arithmetic and religion. It was not regarded as 'primary' to some 'secondary' stage to follow. Indeed the term 'secondary education' was a French expression introduced by Matthew Arnold. Victorians more commonly spoke of 'middle class education' and 'middle class examinations' which more frankly and clearly defined their perceptions of the different kinds of education. Elementary education was an exercise in philanthropy, the religious nurture and social control of the masses, given by the upper to the lower classes. Secondary education was a buyable commodity bought by the middle classes for themselves, the passport to the universities, the professions and back to the family firm.

In these circumstances there was no normal access or flow from elementary to secondary education. Architecture reinforced this. When the Liverpool Collegiate School was built in 1843 as a middle class secondary school and a counterpart of the Bluecoat School for poorer children in the same city, there was no assumption that children would move from one to the other. Even the Collegiate itself was internally divided into three totally separate secondary schools, each for a subtly different level of the middle class, segregated by iron spiked railings in corridor and landing.[2] These assumptions still underlay the 1870 Education Act of W. E. Forster. Under this, School Boards established non-denominational schools to 'fill the gaps' in areas where National (Anglican) and British (Nonconformist) church schools were too distant for children to attend. The assumption was still that the Board Schools were merely elementary schools for the lower classes for whom secondary education was inappropriate.

Elementary education was defined by the seven standards through which all children passed by regular examination. Most children never completed all seven grades but got as far as they could before reaching the school leaving age. The school grant and hence the schoolmasters' salaries depended on the money awarded by the HMIs on the basis of the children's examination results at their appropriate standard. Accordingly the headmaster judged as accurately as possible that standard to which a child's development and attainment most realistically corresponded. So a class of any standard would contain children of quite different ages. Here was a potentially open-ended situation since it was never defined at what age a child had to leave school. Intelligent children could move quite quickly through the standards, and the headmaster had a financial interest in putting them in for the highest HMI's examination they could manage, since passes at higher standards earned more grant money. But the problem arose of what to do with children who had passed through all seven standards before wishing to leave. Indeed, 46 per cent of the children who left Board Schools in York between 1898 and 1900 had reached or passed standard seven.[3]

Headmasters began to devise forms of post-elementary classes in what were called 'higher tops'. Here children who had passed standard seven could be grouped in a separate class or possibly in a small extension to the school for studies not delimited by the Education Department's Codes which specified the grants payable for passes in various subjects. For example, Edmund Rubbra, the future composer, learnt shorthand in these circumstances.[4] In large towns the post-standard-seven children were sometimes so numerous that it was worth taking them from their elementary schools and concentrating them in specially built Higher Grade schools – the origins of the secondary modern schools set up after 1944. Since this was non-elementary work the children could not be financed by the Education Department and accordingly many Higher Grade Schools sought income from the Department of Science and Art in return for teaching a science curriculum. Such schools were known as Organized Science Schools. The actual fabric of the schools remained the responsibility of the School Board under the 1870 Act. It was clear that an anomalous situation was developing. A species of working class post-elementary (possibly secondary) education was emerging, almost as a kind of organic growth, out of the legal and administrative structures designed purely for elementary education.[5] Though of doubtful legality it was responding to a working class yearning for secondary education, which was unlikely to be met through access to the grammar school.

It was just possible to enter grammar school through scholarships even before the new arrangements of the 1900s. With the reform of the grammar school by Lord Taunton's Schools Inquiry Commission and the subsequent Endowed School Commissioners in the 1860s and 1870s, endowments were created for scholarships to enable children from elementary schools to enter grammar schools. Sheffield Grammar School in the 1880s and 1890s had closed scholarships taking three or four boys from elementary schools: sons of joiners, blacksmiths and clerks. Wigan Grammar School had 25 and London as a whole provided some 500 in 1893.[6] On the receiving end, Kennington National School was an elementary school noted in the 1880s and 1890s for winning scholarships to secondary schools.[7] The fixing of the award was a nice problem. A scholarship of less than £25 a year was of little use to the poor, £10 for fees and the rest for maintenance. Awards too low did not attract the working class to compete: awards too high drew in competition from the middle class who could oust those for whom the scholarships were intended. By 1900 there were some 5500 scholarships available.

Some of the more intelligent children could be selected by the headteacher as potential teachers themselves. These pupil teachers received extra tuition from the head and helped him to teach the younger children. It enabled very able working class children to stay on at the elementary school beyond the school leaving age as a stepping stone to teacher training college. Faith Osgerby, the daughter of a stonemason, stayed on at school as a pupil teacher on reaching the age of 13 in 1903 and eventually became a certificated teacher after part-time attendance at Hull Training College. Her exact contemporary, Daisy Cooper, born in 1890, the daughter of a drowned Liverpool sailor, failed to win one of the six scholarships from Liverpool Board Schools to secondary schools. But she stayed at school as a pupil teacher eventually passing to Edge Hill Training College.[8] The importance of the pathway of element- ary school – pupil teacher – training college in creating social mobility for very able working class girls before 1914 can scarcely be exaggerated.

Most children had no opportunity of moving on to secondary levels of education. More typical of the majority was George Tomlinson, the future Minister of Education, who was born in 1890 and became a half-timer at the age of 12, working half a day in school and half in a Lancashire mill. At 13 he left school altogether.[9] His exact contemporary, Jack Lanigan, the orphaned son of a poor Salford engraver, took a School Leaving Examination which was open to fatherless families. To his mother's delight he passed and became an errand boy at the age of 10. James Brady, born in 1898 to a Rochdale clog iron maker, likewise started work before his twelfth birthday through 'sheer force of economic necessity'. Such was the common lot.

For those who could climb higher there was this pseudo-secondary education growing organically out of the structures of elementary schooling. But opinion was divided over the legality and desirability of this. Socialists, especially those on School Boards, favoured any movement to extend the opportunities for working class children, especially those in Higher Grade Schools. The senior civil servant at the Education Department, Sir George Kekewich, was also in favour of these developments, allowing them to grow as a means of creating a working class secondary education system by stealth. Others however, had doubts. The Higher Grade School was of dubious legality and administratively confusing whatever social benefits it conferred. Moreover, some regarded this halfway house as preventing the creation of a full-blown grammar school secondary education system for the lower orders, especially those in Higher Grade schools.

A leading force in this direction was the Royal Commission on Secondary Education (the first use of the term 'Secondary Education' in the title of a government report), under Viscount Bryce which reported in 1895. It took the view that state secondary schools should be created alongside the charitable endowed grammar schools which had been reformed after the Taunton Commission in the 1860s. Whereas these new state secondary schools should be fee paying Bryce recommended that there should be scholarship free places in them for the 'exceptionally able' children from elementary schools. This was in accord with the views of other leading civil servants working under Kekewich. One of them, Sir Michael Sadler, had served on the Bryce Commission and the content of its report owed a great deal to his views. Indeed the setting up of the Bryce Commission was influenced by an earlier conference on secondary education held by Sadler at Oxford in 1893. Sadler ran the Office of Special Inquiries and Reports in the Department which investigated the educational systems of other countries. Studies of European nations confirmed his view that there was a need for a structure in which elementary education would be followed by the secondary stage.[10]

Even more decided in his opinions was Sir Robert Morant who joined the Office of Special Inquiries and Reports as Sadler's assistant in 1895.[11] His own educational background at Winchester and Oxford impressed on him the value of high academic standards. He wished to see new grammar schools in every provincial town bringing some reflection of the qualities of Winchester to a social class of children below that which could attend the public schools. For Morant it was the grammar schools which would diffuse academic values, not the illegal and irrelevant Higher Grade Schools. His study of Switzerland also confirmed his belief in the necessity of an elementary-secondary division. Morant brought from his evangelical background a passionate intensity for reform totally at variance with Kekewich's policy of letting the Higher Grade Schools develop by not interfering with them.

The crisis was brought to a head by the famous Cockerton Judgment of 1899 by which London School Board rate spending on secondary education was declared illegal. This cleared the way for the 1902 Education Act largely masterminded by Morant. Thereby 2568 independent School Boards were abolished and replaced by some 200 Local Education Authorities which were part of the County Councils and County Borough Councils. These LEAs could use the rates to create new grammar schools providing a genuine secondary education leading upwards to the universities and the professions. Kekewich, his support of Higher Grade Schools discredited, retired to be replaced by Morant, and in 1903 Sadler was eased out to a professorship at Manchester. Morant took over the new Board of Education (which the Department had become in 1899) as the most powerful civil servant – 'administrator as statesman' – in education since Sir James Kay Shuttleworth.

The main thrust of Morant's policies lay in the development of the grammar school. In 1904 new Regulations set minimum study times for arts subjects in the new grammar schools. Eight hours a week were to be devoted to English, history, geography and languages and if two languages were to be studied then one had to be Latin. This emphasis on the arts seemed to contradict the contemporary concern for science and technology, yet various considerations lay behind it. In the nineteenth century many schools had boosted their finances by gaining grants from the Science and Art Department in return for teaching science courses and for their pupils' success in science examinations. It was thought that financial inducements had warped the curricular balance of schools to the neglect of the humanities. Morant sought to redress the balance by the 1904 Regulations. Secondly Morant wanted to make the grammar schools genuine ladders for working class children to reach the ancient universities and the learned professions. This role they could only perform by providing the teaching of classics necessary for Oxbridge entrance. To allow the academically able working class pupil into the grammar school and to deny him access to Oxford and Cambridge through the entrance requirements of the classics, would be a cheat. Morant wanted to offer in the grammar school the kind of opportunities he had experienced at Winchester and not the dead end which he saw the higher elementary schools as being. Thus this seemingly reactionary measure was rooted in a profound concern to create possibilities of social mobility for the exceptionally able of the working classes.

The 1904 Regulations were followed by those of 1907 regulating the flow of the lower classes into the grammar schools. The Board policy was that grammar schools should be fee paying but with a system of free places or scholarships for children from the elementary schools. Initially the idea was that 25 per cent of grammar school places should be for these scholarship boys. Scholarships had already risen from 5,500 in 1900 to over 25,000 by 1906.[12] In 1907 Article 20 of the Regulations stated that the proportion of free places 'will ordinarily be 25 per cent of the scholars admitted'.[13] By 1911–12 52,583 children (34.8 per cent) of children in grammar schools were free placers.[14] Most pupils however remained middle class fee payers of very mixed ability. The scholarship Regulations of 1907 were thus a vital part of the ladder of opportunity between the elementary school and the grammar school and a step on the way towards secondary education for all.

Morant was chiefly concerned with the academically highly able and with the grammar schools. Sadler had believed in the desirability of forms of secondary education for less academic children and this had been a matter of contention between Sadler and Morant which lay behind Sadler's departure. Under Morant, a rapid succession of changes began to refashion the policy for secondary education. The Higher Grade Schools, some seventy in number, were taken over by the new Local Education Authorities and about forty were converted into secondary schools. In 1900 the Higher Elementary School Minute allowed for a new type of post-elementary school in which pupils were not allowed to stay beyond the age of 15. At this time schooling was compulsory to 12 (from 1899) though local authorities could (from 1900) require compulsory education until 14. However, there were so many exemptions allowing children to start work early or part-time that the enforcement of a school-leaving age of 14 was not effective until after the Fisher Act in 1918. The new Higher Elementary Schools were intended as an intermediate level between the elementary and secondary schools. By 1905 there were only thirty-five of them, only five of which had been established since 1902. This suggests that thirty of the new Higher Elementary Schools were former Higher Grade School buildings. The Higher Elementary Schools were regarded with suspicion by the Left as a sidetracking cul-de-sac for workers' children. Thus the Higher Elementary Schools did not develop into a strong separate sector of education but were both a vestige of the old School Board system and the seeds of the later secondary modern school.[15]

At a somewhat higher level, local authorities used regulations enabling them to organize day classes for ex-elementary pupils to establish forms of vocational secondary education for the less academic child. These were the Central and Junior Technical Schools. The term Central School had already been used in the 1870s when Sheffield in 1878 had started a Higher Central School, in which it was followed by other major cities. The idea of the Central School was to prepare pupils for commercial and industrial careers and new ones were created for example in London in 1911 and Manchester in 1912. Another variant was the Junior Technical School designed to prepare pupils for more specifically technical occupations than the Central. The Junior Technical came to be recognized as a distinctive form by the Board of Education Regulations of 1913 which enabled them to receive grants.[16]

This brief period of the 1900s was of profound significance in the development of access to education. It saw the origins of a genuinely academic secondary education for the working classes with the possibility of access to the grammar schools. As part of this, the system of selection that was to become the 11+ began here as a competitive rather than a qualifying examination. So too did the notion of a more vocationally orientated secondary education for the less academic child. These ideas of Morant and Sadler were to remain fundamental to the school system for the next half century until the advent of the comprehensive school. As shapers of the pattern of English schooling no civil servants or politicians have been more beneficially influential in this century than Sadler and Morant.

Secondary education for all

In the aftermath of the First World War, the Fisher Act of 1918 improved access to education in two ways.[17] The school-leaving age was raised to 14 and it was then intended that, after that age, young people would continue their education in Continuation Schools. These were to be run by the LEAs for young people at work so that they could receive part-time education under the LEA. The idea was influenced by the German Trade Continuation Schools and publicized before the war by Sadler.[18] The avoidance of an abrupt break between school and work and the interleaving of both activities for teenagers was an important element in the formation of the educated and adaptable German workforce in the nineteenth century. It would also have been especially valuable in England with so limited a system of secondary education for the working classes. Some Continuation Schools were created, but the education cuts in 1921 and 1922 led to the abandoning of the scheme,[19] although one survived in Rugby where it was especially relevant to the local electrical works and their apprentices. This was a major lost opportunity of the twentieth century.

Many policy advocates however were less interested in the Continuation School than in the extension of the right to a secondary education for all children. The Committee on Scholarships drew attention to the fact that the immediate post-war provision of secondary education was insufficient even for those who wanted, and could afford, to avail themselves of it. At the beginning of the school year 1919–20 9,000 boys and girls were excluded, even as potential fee payers, from grant aided secondary schools in England for lack of accommodation.[20] Even worse were the huge potential numbers whom the Committee believed should have been in secondary schools. They reckoned that there were three million children aged 11 to 16 and that of these three-quarters would be 'capable of profiting from secondary education', say 2,250,000 children. Yet pupils in grant aided secondary schools actually totalled only 300,000 with an implied wasted talent of nearly two million young people. Only 9.5 per cent of children in state elementary schools passed on to secondary education. The Committee came to the view that 'the country cannot afford to miss intelligent children', and recommended the raising of the proportion of free place ex-elementary school children in secondary schools to 40 per cent, 'an arbitrary and experimental figure' but a step in the right direction.[21]

The drift in opinion was reinforced by R. H. Tawney of the Labour Advisory Committee in his famous statement of 1922:[22] the old notion of elementary education should be replaced by a system of primary education to be followed by secondary education for all. All should be able to transfer at 11+ from primary to secondary schools and stay there until 16. The Central and Junior Technical Schools should become part of a new system of free and universal secondary education. Tawney called for the abolition of fees in secondary schools and used the raising of the free place allocation to 40 per cent as an interim measure awaiting the expansion of places to provide secondary education for all. The Continuation School had failed. The way forward was universal free secondary education.

This expression of views might have had little significance had not Tawney become an influential member of Sir Henry Hadow's Committee on the Education of the Adolescent which reported in 1926.[23] The Hadow Committee deplored that 55 per cent of children at school between the ages of 11 and 16 were still in elementary schools and that only 7.5 per cent were in secondary and Junior Technical Schools.

Kenneth Lindsay, in the same year as Hadow, had shown the lack of post elementary education experienced by most children throughout the country. Of half a million children who left elementary schools each year only 9.5 per cent proceeded to secondary schools and of these only one-third were non-fee payers, working class children on scholarships. Eighty per cent of children received no education beyond the elementary school.[24]

Hadow called for a break at 11 and a clear division of primary and secondary. He proposed that the term 'primary' would replace 'elementary'. Although educationalists in the 1930s referred to 'primary' education in 'elementary' schools it was not until after 1944 that the 'primary school' replaced the 'elementary school'. Hadow said that 'primary education should be regarded as ending at about the age of 11+. At that age a second stage, which for the moment may be given the colourless name post primary should begin; and this stage which for many pupils would end at 16+, for some at 18 or 19 but for the majority at 14+ or 15+ should be envisaged so far as possible as a single whole within which there will be a variety of types of education supplied.' At the time only 10 per cent of children were actually entered for the 11+ examination. Hadow believed that all children should take the test to present the possibility of a free place to parents and children who might not expect it. He also reiterated the call for the raising of the school-leaving age to 15.

Hadow envisaged a post primary sector of different levels. There would be the grammar school for academic, literary and scientific studies. Modern schools would be created which were to be of a 'realistic or practical trend'. The modern schools were not merely to be inferior forms of secondary school. For whereas the grammar school should cater for a minority of children capable of mastering generalizations and abstract ideas, the modern school should benefit the greater number of children with the ability to do and make, to learn to deal with concrete things and situations rather than book knowledge. 'It should be possible in the case of certain staple industries, such as agriculture, mining, the textile trades and transport, to give the children some knowledge of these industries and of their significance in the national life'. The Junior Technical Schools with entry at 13 would continue and develop though Hadow admitted that in some areas the curricula of these schools would be partially similar to that of the modern schools. It may have been a fault of Hadow to over-emphasize the modern school and to understate the role of the Junior Technical School. He probably over-estimated what could be done with the former and by blurring the distinction beween the modern school and Junior Technical School curricula he failed to give an impetus to selective technological education for able non-academic children. Hadow was realistic about the residual element of the spectrum. He knew that many authorities, before they could afford the reorganization, would have to keep on with 'senior classes' in elementary schools for post-11 year olds. But eventually all-age primary schools would be phased out and replaced with the new structure. LEAs were enjoined to reorganize the old schools and build new ones to reshape the structure to secure a genuine secondary education for all. Selection by differentiation would replace selection by elimination.

The Hadow reorganization was gradually carried out, not so much in the 1920s as in the 1930s. The expansion of school building was helped by the same factors which buoyed the house building boom of the 1930s. The low interest rates enabled local authorities to borrow money very cheaply to build. The low rates of return – or no dividends at all – on equities, prompted investors to seek the safety of local authority bonds. Building materials were cheap, notably Swedish timber, and it was fortunate for Hadow and the LEAs that the subsequent depression paradoxically created circumstances favourable to carrying out the new building necessary to the reorganization.

Accordingly many things changed for the better. Children over 11 were redeployed between the 1920s and 1930s:

Table 10: *The schooling of children over 11 in 1922 and 1937*

| | Pre-Hadow[25] | | Spens[26] | |
	Pupils aged 11–16 in 1922	% of age group	Pupils aged 11–17 in 1937	% of age group
In Elementary Schools	2,014,608	55	1,758,253	43.4
Grant-aided Secondary	264,938	7.2	409,033	9.9
Junior Technical Schools	12,133	0.3	29,431	0.7

There had been an absolute and relative decline of 11-year-olds and over in elementary schools. Yet more striking was the great increase of senior departments in elementary schools taking 163,106 pupils in 1927 rising to 818,827 by 1938.[27] These became barely distinguishable from the modern schools by the late 1930s.

Sir Charles Trevelyan, the President of the Board of Education, encouraged LEAs to increase the proportion of grammar schools' intake from elementary schools from 25 per cent to 40 per cent. The grammar school building expansion increased the chances of getting to a grammar school for children of every social class:[28]

Table 11: *Percentage of children from different social classes attending grammar and independent schools, c.1900–1940s*

% of children going to grammar and independent schools	pre-1910	Children born 1910–19	1920–9
Professional & managerial	37	47	52
Other non-manual and skilled manual	7	13	16
Semi and unskilled	1	4	7

Or as Jean Floud discovered:[29]

Table 12: Percentage of children from different status groups attending grammar or boarding schools, c.1913–42

	% of children born before 1910 and going to grammar or boarding school before 1913	% of children born 1910–29 and going to grammar or boarding school 1921–1942
Status Groups 1–4	27	38
Status Groups 5–7	4	9

Moreover with the Hadow reorganization, the 11+, increased chances of grammar school entry and Hadow's proposed change in terminology from 'elementary' school to 'primary' school, middle class parents came to accept the primary school as the local junior school appropriate for their own children's education. What had been seen in the nineteenth century as the school teaching merely the 'elements' to the lower orders increasingly came to be seen as the normal early stage of most children's education. No longer providing a self-sufficient education it was now simply the primary step to a secondary level to follow. This was exactly what Tawney and Hadow had envisaged.

In the 1920s and 1930s the decision to send a child to a grammar school and the possibility of access depended on a complex of encouraging and inhibiting factors. The chief incentive for working class parents to let their children enter a grammar school, and to keep them there, was the hope of qualifications. These would enable the offspring to enter employment that would safeguard them from the perils of unemployment and poverty which ruined the lives of the unqualified. This was given greater urgency by the institution of the School Certificate in 1917. This was not only the passport to the universities and the higher learned professions but also to the safe and respectable white collar non-graduate opportunities in the banks, building societies, insurance companies and the offices of solicitors, accountants and surveyors. The lower class lad who could break upwards to any of these layers was safe, and might help the family he left behind. The grammar school and the new School Certificate were the keys.

That this should apply to white collar jobs is less surprising than that a similar situation was beginning to emerge over the better quality of craft apprenticeships. The normal age of starting apprenticeships had been the school–leaving age of 14. But with the depression, firms – especially in the less unemployment prone industries – were able to become much more selective and to require a more extended educational background from their applicants for apprenticeships. The age of apprenticeship rose from 14 to 16 which suggests that prestigious firms were not taking modern school leavers of 14 but pupils from Junior Technical Schools and even wooing grammar school pupils with a higher level of basic mathematics. If these were incentives inducing parents to send their children to grammar schools the chief factor making this increasingly possible was the growth of grammar schools them- selves. At the same time there was a fall in the birth rate in the 1920s and 1930s from 24.1 per 1000 in 1913 to 15.1 in 1938, as families responded to the depression by limiting the numbers of their children, to safeguard their standard of living or prevent the outright plunge into poverty. The conjunction of more grammar school building and a declining birth rate increased all classes' chance of attending a grammar school. This was accompanied by increased staying on at school beyond 14, from 7 per cent in 1913–14 to 29.3 per cent by 1936.[30]

Yet for many working class children the balance of adverse factors tipped the scales against getting to the grammar school. Many schools did not encourage their children to think of proceeding to secondary education to avoid the factory, mill and shop. Young Robert Roberts in Salford in 1918 felt a desire to go on learning but his headmaster refused to enter him for a scholarship or give him homework. After abysmally failing an examination in which he entered himself he left his stultifying elementary school and became a tea boy in a brass workshop.[31] Parents too could discourage daughters especially from sitting the 11+ on the grounds that a girl's destiny was marriage and that a grammar school was a waste of time.[32] The more fortunate Ronald Gould (the future knighted leader of the National Union of Teachers) was invited to enter for a scholarship in 1915 which took him to Shepton Mallet grammar school. But he was the only working class boy in his elementary school to be entered.[33]

Further, even when a child of modest means won a scholarship it often had to be rejected since the parents could not afford the hidden costs of stationery, books and uniform. Bim Andrews, raised in poverty in Cambridge, won a scholarship to Cambridge County School in 1920, 'but my mother knew we could not cope with uniform, books, satchel and hockey stick. She was realistic and right.'[34] Miss Andrews went to a Higher Grade School instead. Indeed in Bradford some 60 per cent of free place winners rejected their scholarships.[35] Some children deliberately failed the 11+ and threw away the grammar school place they might have desired, thus taking the shame on themselves rather than present a cruel dilemma to their parents.[36] Most unfortunate were those children denied any schooling at all. In Liverpool in the 1930s Helen Forrester was kept home from the age of 12½ by her impoverished and selfish parents to look after her younger brother and sister. The casual acceptance by the Liverpool authorities of this flagrant disregard of the law infuriated the young girl who yearned for schooling. How many shared her total educational deprivation we cannot know.

The cruelty of the parental dilemma was exacerbated by the circumstances of juvenile employment of the time. Due to anomalies in the insurance system virtually the only people who could be fairly sure of jobs in the 1920s and 1930s were 14- to 15-year-olds. This was because insurance contributions did not begin until the age of 16. This made 14- to 15-year-olds especially and attractively cheap, not only because their wages were low but because the employer faced no liability for insurance stamps. This attractiveness of school leavers in the job market placed greater temptations before working class children to leave as soon as possible. More subtly it acted as a dissuasion from the grammar school since many grammar schools obliged parents to pledge that their children would stay at school beyond the minimum school leaving age of 14. This had no legal force but working class parents were not to know this.

A further factor influencing the flow of children into the grammar schools was the change in the scholarship regulations in 1931. In response to the slump and the need to restrain public expenditure the free places were replaced by 'special' places. Accordingly places in the grammar school were not entirely free to those who passed

Table 14: Percentage of different occupational groups whose children with an IQ of 140+ attended grammar or private secondary schools in the 1930s

Large business owners	100	Skilled wage earners	42.7
Professionals	96.2	Shopkeepers	37
Clerical	57	Unskilled wage earners	32.1

A high degree of misallocation of talent inevitably remained. With around 53 per cent of the intake of grammar schools consisting of highly intelligent selected children, yet this still left around 46 per cent who were there as fee payers having failed or not taken the 11+.[41] The better off could buy the privilege of allocating themselves. This could lead to misallocation as when parents paid fees for offspring to enter grammar schools which their failure in the 11+ had denied them. Here they embarked on academic studies for which they had apparently been proved unsuitable. Conversely there was misallocation as working class children who had passed the 11+ declined their grammar school places for reasons of poverty. In 1935, of highly intelligent children aged 9 to 12½[42] the distribution was as follows:

Table 15: School destinations of highly intelligent children in 1935

40.5% were in elementaty schools aged 9 to 11
19.4% were misallocated by staying behind in elementary schools eleven plus
13.3% were misallocated to Central Schools instead of grammar schools
 8.3% were in grammar schools as scholarship winners
18.5% were in grammar schools paying for themselves

At the end of the 1930s the Spens Report put forward two particular ideas which were to influence thinking about access to education in the future.[43] Sir Will Spens gave an airing to the 'multilateral' school as a way of breaking down the divisions between the grammar school and the modern school of the 1930s. The multilateral school – the forerunner of the comprehensive – would have combined all secondary facilities of the modern, technical and grammar school on a single site focused on some central feature like playing fields. Spens rejected the idea as a plan for general adoption. Indeed since local authorities had recently been spending heavily creating the new buildings of the Hadow reorganization it would have been unrealistic to suggest that they abandon these and embark on even more grandiose construction on fresh sites. Spens also feared that multilateral schools would be too large and that the academic grammar school side would still dominate in prestige over the modern. However the Report encouraged LEAs to experiment with multilaterals especially in areas of new population or in sparsely populated rural areas where the joining of grammar and modern facilities would be feasible. The comprehensive school accordingly entered the field as a policy option.

The other form of schooling which Spens was more keen to advocate was the Junior Technical School. These had grown up before the First World War but had developed only modestly. It was a fault of the Hadow Report that it did not emphasize the importance of this most useful form. By 1938 there were some 248 Junior Technical Schools with 30,000 students,[44] taking only about 5 per cent of elementary school children. Most of them were in London, Lancashire and Yorkshire and indeed a third of County Boroughs had no Junior Technical Schools at all.[45] It was also a defect that entry to these schools was at 13. Grammar school pupils were unlikely to transfer and many modern school children had been given insufficient backing and were already thinking of imminent school leaving by that age. The neglect of the Junior Technical School was one of the worst aspects of the flow of talent in the inter-war years. Spens wanted entry at 11 and an expansion of Junior Technical Schools in line with grammar schools. The war overtook Spens' recommendations but the expansion of the Junior Technical Schools and the initiation of the comprehensive were handed on to the post-war years as possibilities for modifying the flow of ability in the state system.

The 1944 Education Act grew out of a number of considerations.[46] The preceding 1936 Act raising the school leaving age had been nullified by the war and it was expected that after hostilities something similar, at least, would be implemented. The movement behind the Act was buoyed up by strong ideas of 'equality of opportunity', democracy and expectations of extended welfare provision raised by the Beveridge Report of 1942 and to be considered in Chapters III and IV. R. A. Butler himself was determined to transform his role of child minder, to which he had been relegated by Churchill, by some major act of social policy capable of capturing the public imagination. But would this entail any striking rethinking of the pattern of the flow of ability in the system?

The Spens Report of 1938, while suggesting some experimentation with multilaterals and emphasizing the value of the Junior Technical School, envisaged the continuance of the 11+ tripartite division of secondary education according to intelligence. The Green Book of 1941, *Education after the War*, deplored that so many children (13 per cent) even after the Hadow reorganization were still in elementary schools up to 15. It called for equality between the post primary forms of senior school, secondary school and Junior Technical School and the eradication of the falseness of senior schools being still regarded as 'elementary' education.[47] In 1943 Sir Cyril Norwood's Committee believed firmly in the existence of three types of pupil, those 'interested in learning for its own sake', those with 'an uncanny insight into the intricacies of mechanism' and those who 'deal more easily with concrete things rather than ideas'. These rough psychological divisions – abstract, mechanical and concrete – related conveniently to the existing tripartite structure of post-primary education. They concluded, 'accordingly we would advocate that there should be three types of education which we think of as the secondary grammar, the secondary technical, the secondary modern, that each type should have such parity as amenities and conditions can bestow.'[48] Spens, the 1941 Green Book and Norwood all assumed that the Morant–Hadow tripartite system relating to supposed varieties of mental capacities was the best system and, although both Spens and Norwood welcomed some experimentation with multilateral schools, there was no serious expectation that anything other than the tripartite system would be transmitted through the 1944 Act.

The Butler Act was designed to provide education for children according to their 'age, aptitude and ability'. What was new about the Act was not an imaginative restructuring but the abolition of fees in grammar schools. It was hoped that this would create the 'equality of opportunity' which the Act was to embody. It was to remove the anomaly that whereas the grammar schools were supposed to be for 'abstract' thinkers (as Hadow termed it) or those 'interested in learning for its own sake' (in Norwood's definition) yet nearly a half of pupils in grammar schools were there purely as fee payers. Their right to be there depended on the capacity to pay fees, not on some supposed, untested (or failed) intellectual capacity. Spens also deplored that although the grammar school was designed to provide an academic curriculum for pupils proceeding to university,. yet 85 per cent of grammar school pupils did not stay beyond 16. The realities of the situation made nonsense of the belief that types of schooling related to types of intellect in the 1920s and 1930s. They related in fact to a mixture of intellectual and social class characteristics. The great achievement of the 1944 Act was the attempt genuinely to relate the three levels of secondary education to levels of intelligence by excluding the fee payer from the grammar school. In this way access to grammar schools would be limited to those who could pass the 11+, they would all be genuinely 'abstract' thinkers and the failures would no longer be able to buy their way into the grammar schools to confuse the academic concept with a mixed ability clientele.

Otherwise the 1944 Act owed much to earlier thinkers about the system. The unchanged tripartite structure of grammar school, secondary technical and secondary modern were the old grammar school, Junior Technical, higher elementary/central/modern schools reaching back to the 1900s. It was rooted in the thinking of Morant and Sadler transmitted through Hadow and Norwood. The 11+ selection and scholarship looked back to the 1900s and Morant's Regulations of 1907. The assumptions of secondary education for all stemmed from Tawney and Hadow in the 1920s. The 1944 Act was much more a transmitter of the old values and arrangements (1907, 1913, 1922, 1926) of Morant, Sadler, Tawney, Hadow than the radical change it was sometimes regarded as being in the euphoria of the 1940's Welfare State. Whether the flow of talent really was markedly improved by the 1944 Act we shall see in the next chapter.

The public schools

The problems that surrounded the fashioning of a flow of talent through the state system of education did not need to preoccupy the independent sector – the public schools. By the end of the nineteenth century and early twentieth century it was hardly surprising that boys entering such schools came from an upper and upper middle class élite. At the top end of the market Eton had closed ranks and become 'for the first time . . . a school to which only the sons of gentlemen should be admitted'.[49] Indeed, Eton attracted the sons of the governing classes more than any other school prior to 1914 and had become more class exclusive by the 1890s and 1900s than it had been earlier in the nineteenth century. At Winchester, the social origin of boys was likewise elevated:[50]

Table 16: The social origins of boys at Winchester College, 1903–35

Fathers	% of boys born 1890–9 entering school 1903–12	% of boys born 1920–2 entering school 1933–5
Professions	48.6	30.9
Business	14.0	7.5
Forces	18.4	50.8
Government service	7.5	4.2
Gentlemen of leisure	8.9	5.0

The figures in the second column are influenced by fathers still in uniform from the First World War but the high social profile is evident. Eton and Winchester were ancient prestigious schools at the top of the league. Yet well down the scale St Oswald's College, Ellesmere, with modest fees, attracted 68 per cent of its entrants from farmers, the professional and higher business classes.[51] Indeed it was estimated that to pay school fees of around £150 a year a parent must have an income of £1000+ a year. In the 1930s only about ten per cent of incomes were of that level.[53]

The exclusivity of entrance to the public schools was narrowed further by their close connection with the preparatory schools.[54] These had grown up gradually from the mid-nineteenth century partly in response to the increasing tendency of the public schools to select their entry by entrance examinations. By 1900 the self-conscious solidarity of the prep schools and the strength of their connections with the public schools was firmly established. The Association of Headmasters of Preparatory Schools (AHPS) had been founded in 1892 and had 263 member schools by 1899. The inter-relationship of the preparatory and public schools was expressed in various ways. By 1899 there were 343 entrance scholarships from the prep schools to the public schools. A school like Summer Fields in Oxford sent as many as 130 boys to Eton alone in the 1900s. The prep schools also began to shape policy and institutions to their liking in their relationships with the public schools. For example to save young boys travelling to various public schools to take a variety of entrance examinations the Common Entrance Examination was started in 1904 and Greek ceased to be a compulsory element in it from 1908. This co-operative relationship of the junior and senior sections of independent education was especially forged in the 1890s to 1900s. But it had the effect of making it even more difficult to enter public schools, since it was now assumed that a boy had already undergone a preparatory schooling as a prerequisite for Common Entrance. It also greatly increased the expenses to the parent who had to add another five or six years' fees before his son could enter the schoolrooms of Eton or Winchester.

The careers that public school boys adopted also confirmed their élite status:

Table 17: Careers of public school boys, 1890–1939

| | | | Percentage of school leavers | |
| | | | Higher | |
	Professions	Army	business & industry	University entrance
[55]Clifton 1907	22	18	25	39
[55]Marlborough 1906	23	14	23	32
[56]Winchester 1900–10	34.8	28.3	17	consistently
1930–9	33.5	29	18.9	70 (1900–22)
[55]Mill Hill 1907	26	–	32	25
[57]St Oswalds 1890–1903	57	2	24	1
[55]Merchant Taylors 1911	22	11	25	13

As the public schools took their entrants from the higher ranks of society and their pupils in turn moved into lucrative and prestigious positions it was inevitable that public school boys should have been seen to be controlling the 'commanding heights' of the economy and society by the inter-war years. By the late 1920s ex-public school boys constituted the following percentage proportions of leading professions:

Table 18: *Percentages of various professions consisting of ex-public school boys*

	1886–1916	1926[58]	1927	1851–1929[59]	1938	1916–1955
Bishops and Deans		89		90		
Judiciary		77				
Senior Home Civil Servants		72		75		
Indian Civil Service and Dominion Governors		72		71		
Directors of banks and railways		75				
Directors of Courtaulds[60]		60		82		
Cabinet Ministers[61]	67					57

Such a close linkage of the public schools with a narrow clientele of parents, and their pupils' control of key occupations began to attract criticism. T. C. Worsley, an ex-public schoolboy and master accused the schools of being 'a class oligarchy serving class interests' with 90 per cent (he claimed) of their pupils drawn from one economic class.[62] He suggested proposals for the closer integration of the public schools with the state system to enable a widening of the social intake and a tapping of new pools of high intelligence. This was part of the climate of opinion behind the Fleming Report of 1944 which explored these possibilities as we shall see in the next chapter.

The public schools were not entirely disengaged from the state sector in the inter-war years. Most invited inspection from the HMIs, although this was not obligatory except for schools whose teachers participated in the state pension scheme under the Super-annuation Act of 1918. Such participation also entailed an obligation to admit some free place children from LEA elementary schools. This was an interesting technical option which might have increased access to the public schools but it does not seem to have been acted upon. By the end of the 1930s and into the early years of the war the issue of integrating the public schools and the state system gathered importance. Unease was felt over the kind of evidence we have just seen on the social exclusiveness of the schools and the grip of their alumni on leading professions. It was hoped that an influx of pupils from different social origins would leaven the situation.

The public schools also had their own problems. The economic depression of the 1930s had diminished the capacity of their potential clients to pay fees. Moreover the financial hardship and uncertainty had prompted many middle class couples into a 'parents' revolt' of family limitation causing a decline in the birth rate. This too diminished the potential effective demand for fee paying prep and public school education. Indeed 263 prep schools went out of business in the 1930s. If the independent schools could receive some local authority children – the fees subsidised by rates and taxes – it would boost the finances of the private sector. Yet there were also idealistic motives in play. The preoccupation with equality of opportunity and a fairer society that lay behind the movement for the 1944 Education Act also underlay fresh thinking about the public schools as part of the national system.[63]

The universities

If the access to grammar schools and public schools was constrained, that to the universities before the Second World War was inevitably even more selective. In 1900–1 there were some 20,000 university students in Britain with 0.8 per cent of each age group gaining university entrance.[64] By 1914 the figure had risen slightly to 26,711 and the proportion of the age group to about one per cent.[65]

Within these tiny figures there were shades of differences in the social intake. At Cambridge in the second half of the nineteenth century, 1850–99, 31 per cent were sons of churchmen, 19 per cent were sons of landowners, 15 per cent had fathers in business, 10 per cent were sons of doctors and 9 per cent sons of lawyers.[66] The working classes had very little chance of entry. Similarly at Oxford, any yearning Judes remained Obscure and outside. One would expect the social flow into the new civic universities to be somewhat wider since these were intended to serve the industries of their localities and to cater for a wider range of social classes. At Birmingham in 1893 – probably the only year and only civic university for which a detailed breakdown of the intake is possible – the student body came from the following families:[67]

Table 19: The social origins of Josiah Mason College (later Birmingham University) students, 1893

Professional	36.7%
Managerial and manufacturing	16.7%
Lower middle class	33.6%
Artisan working class	12.9%

The working class element was at least there, though small. The lower middle class, small shopkeepers and the like found much greater possibilities of advancement here than at the ancient universities.

In the inter-war years the university population of Britain was around 40,000 in the 1920s and rose steadily between 1926–32 to around 50,000 where it remained fairly constantly throughout the 1930s. This represented a slight upward shift in the proportion of an age group going to university from 1.5 per cent in 1924–5 to 1.7 per cent by 1938–9.[68]

Access to the universities changed slightly. LEAs had been making an attempt to provide scholarships for local students to go to university since 1902 although they had no legal obligation to do so. The young A. L. Rowse, son of a Cornish tin miner, had to win an open scholarship to Oxford in the 1920s before being allocated the only university scholarship awarded by his penny-pinching county.[69] From 1919 state scholarships were awarded for students leaving secondary schools. But only 200 were available, rising to 300 in 1930 and to 360 by 1936 when they became open to all secondary schools and not only to grant aided schools. But with over 4000 school leavers competing for the awards the chances of winning one were slim. Leybourne and White thought that the ratio of applicants to winners was between 16 and 19 to one in the 1930s.[70] Most students had to look to the local authority award as the lubricant for their upward educational mobility. Yet there were problems here. A haphazard system of anomalies had arisen with great variations in the criteria on which awards were based and the value of the awards themselves.[71] A student moving to live outside the area of his award-giving LEA could lose his grant. Provincial universities tended to have contracting arrangements with some LEAs and not with others. Thus if a student lived in a non-contracting area he might be debarred from access to a university of his choice.[72] A critic of the time deploring that less than one per cent of ex-elementary school children reached university observed that 'the possibility of getting educated has come to depend over much on accidents of birth place and residence, and the exact position of the county or county borough boundary has assumed a fortuitous and unreasonable importance.'[73]

The percentage of young people going to university in the 1920s–40s from different social classes was as follows:[74]

Table 20: *Percentage of young people from different social classes going to university, 1920s–40s*

	Children born pre-1910	Children born 1920–9
Professional and managerial	3	6
Non-manual and skilled manual	0.5	1
Semi and unskilled	Nil	0.5

The very low levels of elementary school children reaching the universities attracted comment in the inter-war years. Kenneth Lindsay found in the mid-1920s that only one in 1000 elementary school children reached university or one in 800 in London.[75] In the 1930s the situation seemed only slightly better. In 1933–4 only 0.6 per cent of an age group of elementary school boys reached university whereas 20 per cent of non-elementary school boys did so.[76] This is confirmed by a study of adults in 1949 which found that of persons in the lowest census status groups born before 1910 (and so eligible for higher education in the inter-war years) only 0.9 per cent went to university.[77]

At the end of the 1930s it was pointed out that if the various classes were represented in the universities as they were in society at large then the proportion of state elementary school children in the university population should be 81.1 per cent and of the others 18.9 per cent whereas the actual ratio was 40:60. Professor Greenwood concluded that 'ex-public elementary school children have not quite half and others more than three times their proper share of the university population' and a 'large number of children of ability fit to profit from higher education do not receive it.'[78]

So in spite of the improvements in the access to education in the 40 years from 1900, such imbalances and injustices remained in the system. The war was to be a watershed, but how far would the reforms following it rectify the inequities of the preceding years?

III

Widening Opportunities: Education for All 1944–1985

The 1944 Education Act was to transfer children from primary schools to different secondary schools according to their 'age, aptitude and ability'. In Norwood's terms those of 'abstract' intelligence would go to the grammar schools, the 'concrete' to secondary modern schools and the 'mechanical' to Junior Technical Schools. Yet if it was hoped that the 1944 Act would lead to a greater flow of working class children to grammar schools then these expectations were to be disappointed. Halsey and Floud in their classic study of grammar schools in Middlesbrough and South West Hertfordshire found that there had been surprisingly little change. 'The likelihood that a working class boy will reach a grammar school is not notably greater today, despite all the changes, than it was before 1945. Rather less than ten per cent of working class boys reaching the age of 11 in the years 1931–41 entered selective secondary schools. In 1953 in South West Hertfordshire the proportion was 15.5 per cent and in Middlesbrough 12 per cent.'[1] The difference in class chances of getting to grammar school remained very wide across the spectrum of social classes.

Table 21: Percentage of children from different social classes entering grammar schools, 1953

	S.W. Herts	Middlesbrough
Professionals, business and managers	59	69
Clerical workers	44	37
Foremen, small shopkeepers	30	24
Skilled manual	18	14
Unskilled manual	9	9
All children of all social classes	22	17

Yet could this be regarded as unfair? Halsey and Floud went on to calculate for each location the expected and actual proportion of the respective grammar schools to be composed of working class pupils. This was done on the basis of being able to estimate for any given population what proportion would have an IQ of 114.2, the supposed grammar school entry level.

Table 22: Expected and actual proportions of working class boys in grammar schools, c.1904–18 and 1950s

		Working class boys as a percentage of all boys in the grammar school	
		Expected	Actual
S.W. Herts	1904–18	42	15
	1952	48	51
Middlesbrough	1905–18	40	23
	1953	47	45

Whereas before the First World War, in both localities, the working class were much under-represented in their respective grammar schools, by the early 1950s the expected and actual proportions had come into alignment. Halsey and Floud noted 'the distribution of opportunity stands today in closer relationship to that of ability than ever before'. The proportion of the working class getting to grammar school had risen only slightly since the 1930s: the proportion within a grammar school consisting of working class pupils had risen to levels in according with expectation.

The lack of marked development in the post-war years and the narrower opportunities for the working classes was confirmed in the later major study by A. H. Halsey based on interviews with 8,529 men in 1972.[2] Their chances of attending selective secondary schools were:

Table 23: Percentage of boys of different social classes attending selective secondary schools, 1920s–50s

Birth	1913–22	1923–32	1933–42	1943–52
Enter school	1924–33	1934–43	1944–53	1954–63
% of service (professional) class	69.7	76.7	79.3	66.4
% of working class	20.2	26.1	27.1	21.6

It was interesting that this large national study confirmed the local studies of twenty years earlier. Significant gains were made in the inter-war years but only slight advances after 1944 with the working classes having only a third of the likelihood of selective secondary education of the professional classes.

Yet increasing doubts came to be cast on the fairness of access to the grammar school and the assumptions that children were being efficiently decanted from primary schools into the various categories of secondary school.

First, the great variation in the provision of grammar schools throughout the country made nonsense of the belief that there was some national 'standard' for 'passing' the 11+. Too often access to the grammar school depended not on the child's IQ level but on the available number of places. To an extent this was a legacy of the response to the Hadow reorganization in the 1930s. J. W. B. Douglas showed that the spectrum of possibilities of getting to a grammar school in 1959 was very wide:

Table 24: Regional variations in percentages of all children attending grammar schools, 1959

High chance:	South West 35%, Wales 33.5%, London & S.E. 31.6%
Low chance:	South 18.9%, North East 22.4%, Midlands 24.1%

By making a modest migration between two contiguous areas (South West and centre South) a family could double or halve the chances of its children getting to a selective school.[3] In the grammar schools studied by Frances Stevens the selection rate varied from 40 per cent to 12 per cent of applicants.[4] The school accepting 40 per cent of applicants was too widely selected, leading to problems of early leaving. Dr Stevens considered a selection rate of 24 per cent about right. One of the most extreme cases was Nottingham where in 1954 only 447 grammar school places were available for 4,400 children – only a 10.1 per cent 'pass' rate. That children in some areas had a four times greater or lesser chance than children in others of getting to a grammar school highlighted the unfairness of selection and access to academic secondary education.

Secondly, performance in the 11+ test was shown to be highly dependent on the environment provided by the home. In the case of the working classes this could be detrimental. J. W. B. Douglas selected criteria to indicate parental concern for the child and showed how these varied across the spectrum of the social classes:[6]

Table 25: Differences in the interest in education shown by different social classes

	Middle class mothers		Manual working class mothers	
	Upper m/c	Lower m/c	Upper w/c	Lower w/c
% with high interest in school progress	41.7	21.7	11.4	5.0
Desire for grammar school place	73.3	73.3	57.7	48.8
Wish to keep child at school beyond school leaving age	77.6	40.7	21.7	12.9
Average test scores of children	56.99	53.88	50.08	47.55

The much greater interest and involvement of the upper middle class in all these issues was manifest. This mattered to their children since children whose parents took an interest in their work were encouraged by this to improve their mental ability and test scores between the ages of 8 and 11. Accordingly they benefited directly at the point of taking the 11+ test.

Third, IQ studies showed that intelligence deteriorated in later born children of large families. Three surveys of samples of families of up to six children showed that the youngest child was variously 9.5, 7.8 and 17 per cent less intelligent than the first born. Since it was the working classes who tended to have families of such size, the later born working class children probably faced a further disadvantage in competition with children of small middle class families.

Fourth, doubts were increasingly raised about the nature of the 11+ test. The arithmetic and intelligence parts of the test were believed to be pure tests of mental ability untainted by cultural bias. However, the English part of the test, with its demands for word recognition, wide vocabulary and flexible use of language gave a positive advantage to children from cultured middle class homes. Conversely, working class children surrounded by the restricted patterns of speech of their parents, and lacking the cultural capital

[48]

of books and reading were placed at a disadvantage. The English test, it was argued, was not examining capacity for thought and reasoning but verbal baggage, the possession or lack of which was largely determined by one's parents, home and social class.

There seemed no solution to this problem. Capability in the use of English was a legitimate requirement of the grammar school and had to be tested. Yet however biased the test may have been against the working class the alternative was worse. If the test were abandoned then selection for the grammar school would have to fall back on teachers' assessments. Yet teachers could be influenced favourably by the personality, politeness and appearance of middle class pupils to the extent of over-estimating their ability and under-estimating that of socially poorer children. When the proportion of children whom the teachers *would* have selected for grammar school was compared by Halsey and Floud with the proportion that actually *was* selected on the basis of the 11+ test the divergence is striking:[7]

Table 26: *A comparison of allocation to grammar school by examination and teachers' assessment, 1954*

	% qualified by 11+	% that teachers would have allocated
Professional and managerial	51.1	63.6
Manual skilled and unskilled	12.9	11.5

Whether the test were used, or abandoned in favour of teacher assessment, the bias against the working class seemed manifest and unavoidable.

Unease about the test increased. It was clear that coaching could raise the performance of children, and schools which practised with published test books could give their pupils an advantage.[8] Some candidates could also gain an advantage from the timing of the test. The 11+ was taken by children who would have reached 11 but not 12 on the first of September following the test – which was taken in February. Accordingly children being tested ranged in age from 10/6 to 11/5 and autumn born children gained a slight advantage having been at school for 6 years compared with summer born children who sat after only 5 to 5½ years.[9] The mental development of the latter was also several months behind their older competitors. Girls too tended to be more mature in physical and mental development than boys at the time of the test, while mesomorphs (muscular types) were retarded at 10 to 11 years but advanced quickly in later years.

Furthermore the 11+ test gave no scope for mechanical aptitude testing. Since the 'second cut' of 11+ candidates who just failed the grammar school selection went to Junior Technical Schools this was an especial nonsense. The assumption that a lad who was not quite academic was necessarily mechanical was the dubious basis of this allocation. Tellingly, the 11+ was accused of being good at selecting future clerks, civil servants and schoolteachers but bad at finding future engineers and businessmen.[10]

Moreover there was, of course, no single 11+. Each separate local authority used its own combination of any of 19 or so criteria (intelligence tests, English, general paper, interviews, school records etc.) in a bewildering plethora of variations.[11] The lack of a national test created inevitable differences, some might say unfairnesses, between authorities.

Further unease about the 11+ was created by an awareness that selection was taking place not at 10 or 11 but at a much earlier stage of the primary school. This was through the process of streaming 7- or 8-year-old children into fast and slow classes in their preparation for the examination.[12] This became a self-fulfilling prophecy with the hopes for success and more intensive teaching being invested in the upper stream to the neglect of the lower. Children were not slow to pick up these assumptions about their abilities and futures and responded accordingly. The effect of streaming had the effect of reinforcing the parental encouragement or discouragement which Douglas had shown to be so important an influence on 7- to 11-year-olds preparing for the test. Working class children 'show in particular a severe deterioration in performance if they are put in lower streams'.[13] Moreover the method of streaming was most commonly not by objective tests but by class teachers' recommendations. This likewise tended to favour upper middle class children at the expense of the working class. Brian Jackson in a sample of 252 primary schools using three streams found that over half of children from professional and managerial families were in A streams and nearly half of children from unskilled manual families were in C streams. The class dispersions in 11+ success were already being set several years before.

But the greatest unease about the 11+ was whether it was really an exercise in 'selection' or 'allocation'. To regard it as allocation suggested that the test was genuinely discovering the real 'aptitudes and abilities' of the child before allocating it to the education most appropriate to its needs – academic, technical or modern.[14] These were the ideals and the assumptions behind the operation of the 1944 Act. Yet it was evident by the 1950s that allocation had slipped into selection. It was not a matter of testing a child against a fixed standard but of requiring children to compete severally against each other and all against a limited but highly variable number of grammar school places. The great variation in grammar school places between authorities dominated selection more than pure IQ levels. All these considerations suggested that a considerable misallocation of talent was likely – potential ability denied access to the grammar school, while non-academic minds and many that were failing to develop were trapped inappropriately in grammar schools they yearned to leave at the earliest opportunity.

The misallocation of the potentially able away from the grammar school became evident. Stephen Wiseman found that in 1951 14 per cent of the brightest children in his sample of 14- to 15-year-olds were in secondary modern schools and in 1957 the figure was still 11.2 per cent.[15] Although there were arrangements to transfer able late developers from secondary modern schools to grammar schools at the age of 13, very few benefited from this possibility – only about 2 per cent.[16] Crowther, from his sample of 5,940 National Service Army recruits in the 1950s found that 22 per cent of Army recruits and 29 per cent of RAF recruits had been allocated to schools lower than their ability warranted.[17] Moreover 11+ failures given good teaching and encouragement could so boost their performance as to vitiate the 11+ selection. It was found that 70 per cent of boys who failed the 11+ and who were sent to public school gained five or more passes at O level and a quarter gained two or more passes at A level.[18] Ample evidence was emerging that children of ability, or whose ability developed strongly after the age of 10 were being misallocated by the 11+.

Early leaving

If there was concern about the wastage of ability at the point of 11+ selection, attention was also focused on the waste of those who passed the 11+, went to the grammar school but left early. Either their ability had been overestimated at 10 and they could not cope with academic education, or their high abilities were being squandered by being forced out of the grammar school by home and social pressures. Whatever the reason the flow of talent through the system was vitiated.

The Early Leaving survey found that too high a proportion of pupils was not taking the full advantage of academic grammar school education.[19]

Table 27: Early leaving from grammar schools in the 1940s

	% leaving under 16		% still at grammar school at 18	
	Boys	Girls	Boys	Girls
1945	23.1	25.5	16.7	13.7
1946	23.1	25.6	18.5	15.9
1947	18.4	21.1	21.9	18.5
1948	15.1	17.5	–	–
1949	14.5	17.6	–	–

It was children of lower social groups who tended to leave early. Whereas the semi- and unskilled made up 20.9 per cent of grammar school pupils they made up only 7.3 per cent of sixth forms. Early Leaving saw the home background and parental attitudes as the key factor, 'a boy whose father is of professional or managerial standing is more likely to find his home circumstances favourable to the demands of grammar school work than one whose father is an unskilled or semi-skilled worker. The latter is handicapped.'[20] They were handicapped by overcrowding, social assumptions or shortage of money – to a lesser extent: it seems that only 11 per cent of early-leaving boys and 18 per cent of girls left early because their parents could not afford to keep them on.

A specific study of early leaving from Southampton grammar schools in the early 1950s found that the chief reasons for this were:[21]

Table 28: Reasons for early leaving from Southampton grammar schools, 1950s

Low ability	31.7%
Home conditions	30.2%
No will to work	20.1%
Wanting an early career	17.8%

It was sad that most left for negative reasons and over half left for reasons which suggested that they had been over-optimistically allocated to grammar schools at 11+. Early leavers left for clerical and office careers, and apprenticeships – all worthwhile outcomes, but not the most appropriate use of the highly academic/scientific education of the 1950s grammar school.

As the importance of staying on began to dawn on all classes by the late 1950s, so early leaving before 16 declined from the 23 to 25 per cent levels of the 1940s to 11 per cent by 1958–9.[22] In the jargon of the day, the 'trend' to staying on swelled sixth forms as parents of all classes enjoyed the full employment and prosperity of the 1950s and hopefully looked to university entrance for their offspring as the gateway to a qualified and secure career. Accordingly the number of boys and girls in sixth forms rose between 1947 and 1958 from 32,000 to 53,000 an increase of 66 per cent.[23] This was all the more remarkable in that these were children born *before* the birth rate bulge of the mid-1940s. The early leaving problem receded before that of the advancing trend.

However, the problem of the underachievement of children from the lower classes in the grammar school continued to cause anxiety. Some argued that there was a fundamental clash of cultural values between the grammar schools and their working class intake. The grammar school values were those of 'hard work, ambition, good sense and strict morality' laced with some public school virtues 'scholarly accomplishment, social poise, athletic prowess and leadership'.[24] Many of the working class did not wish to measure up to this or found such values at variance with those of the home. The grammar school encouraged rugby rather than soccer, homework rather than leisure and both in preference to the 'youth club'. Indeed the grammar school was concerned to defend its values against those of the prevalent popular youth culture.

The limited success of working class children in the grammar schools became apparent. At 'Hightown' (a pseudonym for a

North of England grammar school), a highly selective grammar school taking only 15 to 20 per cent of 11-year-olds, major social class differences emerged:[25]

Table 29: Educational achievements of different social classes at 'Hightown' grammar school, 1962–5 (percentages)

1962–5	No O levels	Staying into 6th form	3 A levels
Upper middle class	11.0	73.0	56.0
Working class	23.4	47.4	27.3

In spite of their high intelligence working class boys were not flowing through the grammar school as effectively as their abilities would warrant. Colin Lacey indicates that family backgrounds had still a powerful influence in advancing or retarding pupils' performance. 'The school is seen as a competitive arena in which teams consisting of the pupil and his parents compete for scarce rewards such as examination success.'[26]

A study of Huddersfield confirmed the disproportionate under-performance of the lower classes:[27]

Table 30: Proportions of children from different social classes taking A levels in Huddersfield

Huddersfield social structure		Leaving grammar school after taking A levels
% of professional, clerical	22	64
% of skilled, unskilled manual	78	36

Huddersfield with a population of 130,000 sent only 38 working class boys from grammar school to university in a four-year period in the 1950s. Working class pupils and their parents tended to be ignorant about university entrance and grants while girls especially could be diverted to teacher training colleges. Working class success in the grammar school in Huddersfield was associated with small families living near a successful primary school with parents who were 'sunken' middle class. These were parents of middle class origins who had sunk economically into a lower class but retained many of their original values. This was combined with a fierce concern that the next generation would regain middle class status through the grammar school.

If these were characteristics of working class success in the grammar school those of failure were equally plain. The factors were already there by the end of the first year. R. R. Dale found that 36 children improving their performance were in social classes 2 to 5; 37 deteriorators were in social classes 5 to 7. The large family was a stifler. 'Not only is a large family more likely to draw near the poverty line and therefore be unable to pay for facilities such as books and the comfort of a fire for homework, but also interruption by other children may help substantially to the deterioration of a grammar school pupil . . . Nor can the parents give as much attention to any one of five or six children as to an only child.'[28] Most telling was the parents' own educational background: 'in only one case amongst the deteriorators was there a parent educated in a grammar school'. The working class grammar student, unlikely to have a grammar school parent, lacked the understanding support necessary for success. The failures in Dale's case histories experienced messy lives of no home culture, poverty, neglect, excessive travel, illness and trivial social distraction which were destroying their academic performance.

J. W. B. Douglas summed up the situation: 'three times as many middle as lower manual working class pupils stayed on at school till the end of 1961–2 session (i.e. until 16) whereas on their measured ability and the quality of school they attend only one and a half times as many would be expected to do so. Similarly four times as many middle class pupils get an O level certificate whereas only twice as many would be expected to achieve this. On each criterion then, the fact of being middle class roughly doubles the chances of educational success.'[29] There was too much misallocation of talent, too many extraneous factors impeding the efficient flow of ability, too close a relationship of selection and success with social class background.

The secondary modern schools

Whatever the problems of access to the grammar school and the performance of working class pupils there, the 1944 Act left the secondary modern school in a highly unsatisfactory position. It had to take some 75 per cent of primary school leavers or some 70 per cent of all 11-year-olds. Yet pupils arrived at the schools with the stigma of having 'failed' the 11+. The notion of running an education system in which nearly three quarters of the population have already 'failed' at the age of 11 is curious to say the least. The mythology was that children went to secondary modern schools because they had special 'concrete' attributes tested by the 11+. In fact the positive possession of these concrete attributes was only a negative presupposition of their proven lack of academic (grammar school) capabilities. It transmitted itself in attitudes. Edward Blishen found his boys at Stonehill Street Secondary Modern School as 'sulky, vicious, less like boys than ruined men' who 'hated school with a coarse sullen hatred.'[30] The public at large associated the new secondary moderns with the old Hadow 'senior classes' and modern schools of the 1920s and the older higher elementary schools of the 1900s – still a form of extended elementary education for the working classes by another name. Between 1945 and 1956 536 new secondary modern schools were built.[31] But there were 3,872 secondary modern schools in England and Wales teaching 1.5m children in 1961.[32] In addition there were 1,026 all-age schools still unreorganized since Hadow. In all there were some 5,000 buildings providing secondary modern education only 10 per cent of which were new and purpose built. Most were old and carried with them the historical resonances of working class pseudo-secondary education. Moreover only a fifth of their teachers were graduates, receiving lower incomes and fewer resources than grammar school teachers. In these circumstances it was difficult to sustain the hopes of Norwood that there would be a 'parity of esteem' between the post-1944 forms of schooling.[33]

The social class of the intake into secondary modern schools was biased towards the lower end:[34]

Table 31: Social class of pupils in secondary modern schools, 1950s

	% of intake
Professional, managerial, clerical	14
Skilled manual	55
Semi and unskilled	31

The Newsom Report presented this social imbalance of intake graphically in terms of three imaginary families, the Browns, Jones and Robinsons. The Browns were the top quarter of ability, the Jones the middle two quarters and the Robinsons the lowest quarter.[35]

Table 32: Social class and ability ranges, 1963

Social class %	Ability ranges		
	Brown	Jones	Robinson
Professional & managerial	7	4	2
Clerical	11	9	7
Skilled manual	59	55	53
Semi-skilled	14	16	18
Unskilled	9	16	20
Likely to stay into	John Mary	John Mary	John Mary
the sixth form	42 43	16 19	3 4

Much heroic work was achieved. H. C. Dent surveying secondary modern schools in the mid 1950s found 52 per cent doing good work of originality, 43 per cent doing sound work and only 5 per cent positively bad.[36] In the 1950s their pupils were increasingly entered for GCE examinations, rising from 4,068 in 1953 to 22,000 by 1960.[37] To cater for children below GCE level in subject areas of interest to employers the CSE was started in 1965. Dent was sure of 'the incontestable fact that by 1957 hundreds of thousands of girls and boys in secondary modern schools were being given a much better, much more genuinely secondary education than were even their elder sisters or brothers who attended the self same schools only a few years previously.'[38]

Fundamentally what was wrong with the secondary modern schools was not inadequate buildings, staff or pupils but the disintegration of a feebly thought out concept. As William Taylor noted, 'the attempt to create a *distinctive* type of modern school education was foredoomed to failure.'[39] In truth there was no clear view of what was conceived of as a residual category after the clearer divisions of (grammar school) 'academic' and (Junior Technical School) 'mechanical' had been creamed off. Yet this was a residuum consisting of the vast bulk of the nation's children.

Moreover such were the geographical inequalities and psychological inadequacies of selection that sizeable proportions of academic and practical intelligence were allocated to the modern schools. The consequence was that they began to spread over a wide spectrum of purpose and activity. They ranged from Blishen's dreadful 'roaring boys' to those moving into the grammar school sphere with GCE work and into the technical school sphere with craft and engineering courses. How far the modern schools should be 'practical' or 'realistic' without being 'vocational' was a matter of almost theological distinction. There always had been a tendency from the 1880s and 1890s for the historical predecessors of the secondary modern schools – the higher elementary schools – to extend their curriculum in imitation of socially and academically superior schools. The modern schools of the 1950s were doing the same. They were helped by the flood of pupils provided by the birth bulge, many able ones being excluded from the grammar schools in the fierce competition. Also, it became clear that Junior Technical Schools were not to be expanded as part of the tripartite structure. Accordingly, modern schools moved into this territory with courses in building, auto-engineering and so forth. In the 1950s and 1960s many large modern schools were combining the functions of grammar school and technical school. Whatever the distinctive idea of the modern school had been, it was becoming very unclear at this time. It was but a step to regarding the modern school as the precursor of the comprehensive, which would truly combine in one institution the range of functions which the modern schools were already assuming with non-selected pupils.

The Secondary Technical School – the lost opportunity

The third part of the tripartite structure was the Junior Technical School, now, after 1944, renamed Secondary Technical Schools. Whereas there were too many secondary modern schools dealing with too widely disparate an ability range, the problem of the Junior Technical School in the flow of ability was that there were far too few of them. Secondary modern schools took about 70 per cent of children, grammar schools about 20 per cent, the independent schools about 5 per cent, but Secondary Technical Schools merely 3 or 4 per cent. There was a complete imbalance in the flow of children into the three parts of state secondary education.

The Junior Technical Schools had developed in the 1900s and were recognized by the Minutes of 1913. In the Hadow proposals they remained firmly one of the three main forms of new secondary education although the Hadow Report (1926) did not stress their importance as much as it might have done. It was a damaging anomaly that the Junior Technical Schools' age of entry was 13, unlike 11 for other forms of secondary education. This meant that children did not automatically move into them from elementary school. They would have attended some other school first, usually a central school. An intake age of 13 also assumed that children were prepared to stay until 15, a year later than the school-leaving age of 14. The two-year span also entailed that there would be relatively few schools and pupils in them:

1929	108 Junior Technical Schools	18,000 pupils
1938	248 Junior Technical Schools	30,457 pupils[40]

Most of these were in London, Lancashire and Yorkshire. Indeed a third of local authorities had no Junior Technical Schools at all by the end of the 1930s, as we have seen.

Moreover pupils leaving Junior Technical Schools at 15 had a year's gap before being able to enter technical college at 16. This they had to spend in industry or at evening classes. This was all the odder in that Junior Technical Schools were often in the same building as the technical college. Things were also not entirely ideal within the junior techs. Although their intention was to raise the standards of the British technician and craftsman, some had excessively academic pretensions, teaching French for university entrance for example. Richardson noted that 'most of the pupils who have passed through these schools find their way ultimately into the higher grades of industry and to such an extent that only 9 per cent have remained in the ranks of craftsmen.'[41] While it was excellent that young men were moving ahead, this comment suggests that the Junior Technical Schools were picking up too many who in a fairer and more efficient system would have been in grammar schools and universities.

The Spens Report was strongly in favour of a considerable expansion of Junior Technical Schools and deplored that Hadow had rather neglected this aspect and that admissions to these schools were only a tenth of those to grammar schools. Spens wanted the age of entry to be reduced to 11 and greater parity of size and prestige between the junior technical and grammar sectors. Norwood, the 1941 Green Book and 1943 White Paper assumed that Junior Technical Schools would be continued as part of the tripartite system after the 1944 Act. They were in favour of them without giving them that special boost which Spens would have wished.

The 1944 Act lowered the age of entry to Junior Technical Schools to 11 as Spens suggested though this raised doubts over whether technical ability could be detected at 11 or distinguished from all round general ability. Possibly to avoid putting children into specialized Junior Technical Schools, some authorities developed a bilateral approach having grammar technical or technical modern schools with a technical stream in one of the other more popular forms. Only 63 new secondary technical schools (now so-called) were created between 1945 and 1960 but their overall number declined from 319 in 1948 to 266 by 1960, about the same level as in the 1930s. [42]

This was a great pity since it was evident from studies in the mid-1950s just how valuable these schools were. Not only were they teaching subjects of direct relevance to employment and providing the scarce skills which industry needed, but they inculcated more positive attitudes even than grammar schools. Technical schoolboys were much more work orientated, they felt that they were already starting their careers, expected high job satisfaction and had a strong belief that ambition could be fulfilled by hard work. Boys in technical schools held these views more strongly than grammar or modern boys. [43]

The failure to develop the junior technical and secondary technical schools is perhaps the greatest lost opportunity of twentieth century English education. Since 1944 the grammar schools with their academic and pure science values have had a disproportionate prestige compared with their technical counterparts preparing young people for the work of productive industry. Many working class pupils disenchanted with the grammar school might well have had happier or more fruitful careers in technical schools. It has been said that 'what the working class gained through the expansion of the grammar schools they very largely lost through the decline of the technical schools'.[44] Also, there were far too many pupils across too wide a spectrum of ability allocated to secondary modern schools. The technical schools should have been developed much more beyond this 3 or 4 per cent, and remained closely linked to technical colleges and industry. That they were not is a major cause of the chronic shortage of skilled labour which British industry has suffered since 1945.

Demands for the comprehensive school

Such were the difficulties and anomalies behind the swing of opinion towards comprehensive schools: the difficulties of the working class getting to the grammar school and their under-performance there, the excessive range of ability in secondary modern schools, the absurdity of condemning 75 per cent of the population to failure at 11; the inadequate provision of technical education at school level.[45] The hope that total fairness would be achieved by the abolition of fee paying in the grammar school proved unfounded. Too much of the legacy of social and educational division going back to the 1900s was transmitted through the Butler Act and there were too many social factors slewing and eddying the flow of ability from its appropriate destination. The selection at 11+ was too uncertain and too final. The only solution seemed to many the new form of comprehensive school, abolishing selection at 11 and sending all children to the same school. Here their disparate and changing abilities could be catered for as they developed, without the stigma of 'passing' or 'failing' which had confused the allocation of ability.

Since Spens a few influential voices were raised in favour of the multilateral school, but the assumptions of Norwood, the 1941 Green Book and 1943 White Paper, and hence the 1944 Act were in

favour of the tripartite system. The policies of the Labour governments of 1945–51 were in accord with this and hence LEAs
implemented the 1944 Act on tripartite lines. There were some
early pioneers: Windermere in 1945, Anglesey in 1949 with
Kidbrooke in London as the first purpose-built comprehensive in
1954.[46] The increasing unease about selection and other matters
expressed in writings of the 1950s and 1960s, some of which we
have seen in the last few pages, caused LEAs to think of new
structures – sixth form colleges, the Leicestershire Plan with a
break at 14 and the option of a move, without selection, to a
grammar school.

Comprehensive schools themselves developed even under the
Conservatives. In 1954 there were thirteen, rising to 195 by 1964.
The Conservative governments of the 1950s were not generally in
favour of comprehensives, preferring the grammar school. But
they were prepared to sanction comprehensives as experiments in
new housing estates or in rural areas where they would be focal
points of thinly scattered populations. In 1964 Labour returned,
now committed to encourage comprehensives and in 1965 Anthony
Crosland issued his Circular 10/65 (12 July 1965) requesting LEAs
to make comprehensive schools the normal pattern within five
years. The system expanded:

Table 33: The expansion of comprehensive schools 1965–70

	Comprehensive pupils	As % of all secondary students	Comprehensive schools
1965	240,000	8	262
1970	937,000	30	1145

Circular 10/65 gave a wide choice to LEAs in how they interpreted
the organization of comprehensive schools. The basic idea was to
abolish selection at 11+ and the allocation to the tripartite system
on the basis of this. Within this there were considerable variations.
Two thirds included sixth forms, a third had a break at 16 and then
transferred pupils to sixth form colleges. Some comprehensives
abolished any streaming and tried mixed ability classes, others set
pupils in ranked sets according to ability.[47]

In 1970 the Conservatives returned with Margaret Thatcher as

Secretary of State for Education and Science. She withdrew 10/65 with her Circular 10/70. This reversed Crosland's policy and envisaged comprehensives co-existing with grammar schools which the Conservatives wished to protect. In 1974 Labour returned again in the February and October General Elections with Reg Prentice keen on pushing on with comprehensivization. He abolished the direct grant schools in 1975 hoping to force many to go comprehensive, although the outcome was that the vast majority became independent. Accordingly the Conservative government of 1979 was presented with an educational system in which comprehensives had become the predominant state sector form.

It might be thought that with all children in the state sector (about 94 per cent of all children) passing without selection from primary to comprehensive that perfect equality of opportunity had been achieved. But not so. Firstly, although the creation of comprehensive schools had largely eroded the tripartite system, grammar schools still remained. There were still 893 grammar schools in 1972 and Mrs Thatcher in her three and a half years at the Department of Education disallowed 92 cases of comprehensivization where a grammar school would have been absorbed. There were still some 400 grammar schools in 1978, on the eve of the Conservatives' return. In 1987 157 remain. This co-existence of grammar schools and comprehensives posed problems. Anthony Crosland ('If it is the last thing I do, I'm going to destroy every grammar school in England')[48] was clear that grammar schools and comprehensives could not co-exist, with the former creaming off the more gifted children from the latter. Dame Mary Green starting Kidbrooke was hindered by the retention of nearby Eltham Hill Grammar School which deprived her of a grammar school element. In Newcastle in the 1980s six independent schools still cream off the middle classes of high ability which risks reducing local comprehensives to secondary moderns.

This practice has, from the start, undermined one of the assumptions of the comprehensives, that they were supposed to have 20 per cent of their intake in each of five levels of intelligence. Risinghill in Islington, which closed amid lurid publicity in 1965 had 81.5 per cent of its pupils in the lowest ability groups 4 and 5.[49] Rhodes Boyson's Highbury Grove,[50] which opened in Islington in 1967, two years after Risinghill had closed, found the same problem.

It was denied a spread of ability across the intake, having to take 20 per cent of high ability and 40 per cent of low ability. This prevented a genuinely comprehensive school of mixed abilities. The imbalance arose from nearby grammar schools creaming off the higher ability children of the area. It is interesting that Boyson's experience confirmed Crosland's 1960s view that comprehensive and grammar schools could not co-exist without detriment to the former.

Second, the comprehensives could not remove those characteristics of disadvantage in society at large which affected children's response to education. Although the education offered to children, disadvantaged or not, was now the same, their domestic circumstances continued to affect the child's response to that education. Of disadvantaged children (one parent or large family also poorly housed and of low income) only 41 per cent hoped to continue any education after 16 compared with 71 per cent of their peers. Their reading and calculation was poorer and they stood a high risk of not even being entered for the CSE and GCE. It was estimated that there were 500,000 of these children under 16 in 1974 and for them secondary education, whatever its structure, could not obviate the harmful effects of homes and incomes.[51]

Finally some critics have argued that the comprehensives have failed to alter the basic defects of the old secondary modern system. Children in comprehensives tended to have friendships with children of their own social class. Comprehensives did not widen cross-class friendships as much as grammar schools nor did they widen the career aspirations of working class children. Most importantly, having academic, technical, modern streams in comprehensives merely reproduced the tripartite system they were supposed to replace. Given the retention of streams, able working class children were more likely to do well in pure grammar schools than in the academic streams of comprehensives. Julienne Ford concluded that there was little evidence that comprehensive education 'will modify the characteristic association between social class and educational achievement' and 'the notion that social structures can be changed through educational reform is a liberal myth.'[52]

The public schools, from Fleming to Assisted Places

If the war years marked significant change in access to secondary education in the state sector so, too, many hoped that they would initiate changes in access to the public schools of the independent sector. The problem of transferring elementary schoolboys to public schools with free places had been raised as early as 1919 by Sir Frank Fletcher, the chairman of the Headmasters' Conference. Twenty years later the HMC and representatives of the governing bodies of the public schools (the Governing Bodies Association formed in 1941) started meeting to discuss the future of the public schools. Accordingly in July 1942 it was in response to representations from the HMC and GBA that R. A. Butler, the President of the Board of Education, set up the Fleming Committee to consider means 'whereby the association between the public schools . . . and the general education system of the country could be developed and extended.'

Lord Fleming, a Scottish judge, took the view that public schools had not created the social divisions of the nineteenth century: 'They were in fact called into being to meet the demands of a society already deeply divided.' Yet if the divisions had arisen for other economic and social reasons he admitted that the public schools had reinforced them, 'it may almost be said that nothing could have been better devised to perpetuate them [the divisions] than this educational development'.[53] In fact, although Fleming did not make the point, the Victorian public schools had a strongly cohesive as well as divisive effect. They effectively absorbed the new professional and business classes into a new more richly varied élite than the landed aristocracy they replaced. It was accordingly quite feasible to envisage the public schools being able to absorb a limited number of pupils from the state sector. Fleming himself deplored 'the unreality of an educational system which segregates so thoroughly the boys of one class from those of another.'[54]

The Fleming Report in 1944 made various proposals to facilitate the transfer of children from the state sector to the public schools. Under Scheme A pupils thought able to profit could be sent by their LEA to a public school on an approved list. The LEA would pay for the costs of the schooling and could make some charge to the parents according to their income. Under Scheme B the Board of Education itself could grant bursaries to qualified pupils who had already been educated for at least two years in grant aided elementary schools. Schools in the scheme would offer one quarter of their places to former state pupils. We need not linger over the details since so little materialized from them. Why was this?

The Fleming proposals were baulked by various problems. Not least were the personal difficulties which could be experienced by the 'guinea pig' pupils pitched into the unfamiliar world of the public school. These were imaginatively explored and brought to a wide popular audience by the Boulting brothers' film *The Guinea Pig* in 1948.[55] Here 'Jack Read' (played by Richard Attenborough) was depicted as the son of a lower middle class tobacconist sent from his elementary school by the gas works to 'Saintbury' school on a scholarship provided by the public school itself. Described as a 'complete street oik' he lacks not only Latin and French but any kind of social assurance. His housemaster is hostile to the working classes, 'Jack' hates the snobbery of the school but feels *déclassé* and uncomfortable at home, his parents feel embarrassed at visiting the school. Out of this maelstrom of class tensions 'Jack' wins through, acquiring self confidence, team spirit and a scholarship to Cambridge. This was in truth quite realistic. A group of real life 'guinea pigs', interviewed forty years on, valued the improvement to their lives brought about by their being sent to public schools in the immediate post–Fleming years.[56]

The Fleming scheme ultimately failed not because the 'Jack Reads' could not cope but because administrative and financial difficulties obstructed the flow of ability. One thousand assisted places a year were offered by the public schools and indeed many schools welcomed the scheme, feeling that they had nothing to lose. Rugby provided two places a year for Hertfordshire and Mill Hill offered places to Middlesex. Reciprocally some LEAs were eager to respond. Jack Longland, when Chief Education Officer of Dorset, was one of the first, sending two boys to Eton. Hertfordshire sent boys not only to Rugby but to Eton and Winchester also. It tended to be Conservative LEAs who were most keen on the Fleming scheme. But most were suspicious or apathetic and it was on the reluctance of the LEAs rather than the aloofness of the public schools that the Fleming scheme foundered.

First, it became clear that the state would not help with fees as was originally planned and that all the costs would fall on the LEA and parents. Second, many Labour LEAs were suspicious that the scheme was merely a disguised way of helping the finances of the public schools after their difficulties in the financially straitened and low birth rate 1930s. Subsidizing the schools of the rich out of sums paid by modest ratepayers was difficult to justify. Third, most LEAs came to see that the best way in which they could help their ablest working class children was through the development of first rate LEA grammar schools. By the 1950s in any case it was less evident than in the 1930s and 1940s that public schools were greatly superior to grammar schools in the state sector. Finally by the 1950s the public schools were in a buoyant condition and had no real financial need of handfuls of subsidized, possibly socially problematic, children from the local authorities. In these circumstances the hopes of 25 per cent of public school places being offered to and accepted by local authorities came to be increasingly unrealistic and the scheme petered out. As a bold scheme to engineer a greater flow of talent up the system the Fleming proposals were a failure. But it has left behind a handful of men (like the son of a miner whose father paid 20 per cent of his income to send him to Shrewsbury) deeply appreciative of the unusual privileges which have transformed their lives.

With the petering out of the Fleming scheme the public schools embarked on a sustained flourishing period underpinned by the long post-war boom. Yet if there was no leavening of a working class element as Fleming had hoped, there were significant shifts within the monied classes who could afford private education. In particular some deplored that the traditional professional classes were finding greater difficulty in affording public school fees and were being replaced by the business classes. 'Mr Chips' of 'Brookfield School' was already deprecating the advent of the sons of 'financiers, company promoters, pill manufacturers'.[57] By the 1950s these new parents were welcomed by one headmaster as 'the rapidly expanding technical and managerial class which is increasingly indispensable in the age of automation and technological development and which commands in consequence the highest salaries'.[58] This became evident from surveys of the social origins of public school boys:

Table 34: The social origins of public schoolboys, 1959, 1960s

	% of pupils at Ardingley 1959[59]		% in an Eton House 1960s[60]	Graham Kalton's survey 1962–3[61]
Business	51	Industry and commerce	38.9	
Professional	24		25	32
Scientists	20			
Armed Forces	4		5.6	
Farmers	3		19.4	
Skilled non-manual				5
Skilled manual				2
Semi-skilled				1

Ian Weinberg studying fifteen public schools found that 'business-men comprised the largest group of parents' though in the very best schools 'the professionals are holding their own against the competition of businessmen'. Lawyers and doctors were 'solidly represented' with 'a fair number' of Administrative Class civil servants. By contrast, the financially declining professions of the clergy and teaching 'hardly appear among parents'.[62] Many welcomed the substantial proportions of businessmen and scientists as reflecting the public schools' capacity to respond to the changing dispositions of wealth in society.

Various factors lay behind this slight shift in the flow. The 1944 Act denied wealthy 11+ failures the option of entering the local grammar school as fee payers. Resort to the independent sector became their alternative to the secondary modern. The public schools themselves became more attractive with a greater emphasis on science. This was encouraged by the establishment of the Industrial Fund for the Advancement of Scientific Education in 1955. By 1957 141 companies had subscribed over £3m for scientific laboratories and education in the public schools.[63] Accordingly by 1959 over a half of public school sixth formers were studying science and mathematics.[64] Firms not only encouraged the schools but also helped the parents, with an increasing number of employers providing assistance with school fees for managerial employees as a tax avoidance fringe benefit.

In their intakes the public schools were creating a self-perpetuating élite leavened by a rich admixture of new business money. Many public schoolboys were sons of public schoolboys by the 1960s. In two of Weinberg's schools 30 per cent and 33 per cent of fathers of pupils were old boys,[65] at Haileybury it was 25 per cent; Kalton likewise found that 21 per cent of all pupils of independent boarding schools were following their fathers to the same school while 52 per cent of boys at boarding schools had fathers who were ex-public schoolboys.[66] At Harrow four fifths of the boys in one house were sons of Harrovians.[67] At Eton a housemaster noted that 'practically all applications [for entry] come from men who were themselves at public schools and the majority from old Etonians'. In fact half of the fathers of boys at McConnell's House were old Etonians.[68] At girls' public schools likewise some 55 per cent of girls had ex-public school fathers.[69] A perceptive young lad at prep school sensed the point behind the figures: 'I think it is pretty well first class people that go to a public school, not the actual workers' sons, but the bloke that is in charge, his sons. It is the sons of the important men really who come to a school like this.'[70]

If the schools were creating a self-perpetuating élite through their intake there was continued concern over the future positions of their output. The dominance of ex-public schoolboys in leading occupations, highlighted in the 1920s, were also evident in the 1960s.[71] Ex-public schoolboys made up:

Table 35: Proportion of various occupations consisting of ex-public schoolboys, 1960s

Over 50% of Admirals, Generals and Air Chief Marshals
Over 60% of physicians and surgeons at London Teaching Hospitals
      and on the GMC
Over 70% of Conservative MPs
Over 80% of judges and QCs, directors of prominent firms,
      Governors and Directors of the Bank of England,
      Church of England Bishops
Over 90% of the Conservative Cabinet of 1967

It seemed to one commentator that 'the sociological function of the public schools is to support a particular social class'.[72]

Partly for this reason the public schools in the 1960s and 1970s came under various pressures to which they responded creatively in ways which have been termed a 'public school revolution'.[73] The Labour government from 1964, concerned about the supposed divisive and élitist nature of the public schools, determined to integrate the public schools into the state system and abolish their independent status. This appeared for the first time in the 1964 Labour manifesto and reappeared in 1974 as a pledge to withdraw their charitable status. A Public Schools Commission was appointed in 1965 to consider the integration of the schools. They envisaged 45,000 assisted places organized by a national and not merely LEA scheme. The lack of outcome of these proposals prompted many Labour politicians to think that total abolition was the only alternative. Meanwhile, the inflationary crisis of 1973–9 quadrupled the cost of fees in independent schools from an average £545 in 1966 to £2,744 by 1980. This led to fear that they would price themselves beyond their clients' means – a fear as unfoundedly pessimistic as the 45,000 proposed assisted places proved optimistic. In fact the proportion of the male population receiving a public school education rose from 4 to 5 per cent in the inter-war years to a steady 7 per cent since the Second World War.[74]

The public schools responded to these pressures in various ways. The swing towards science, encouraged by the Industrial Fund, continued. Half the public schoolboys going to university in 1980 were studying engineering, science or medicine. John Rae noted of his Westminster boys, 'the time British public school boys once spent writing Latin verses is now spent writing computer programs'.[75] It was in keeping with the now large business element among parents. The swing to science took place in a context of improved academic standards in the public schools. There was less concern about 'blues' among the staff and more about 'firsts' and PhDs. By 1979 independent schools won 64 per cent of the open awards to Oxford and Cambridge and the leading handful (Dulwich, Winchester, Westminster, Eton, St Pauls) each regularly won 50 places at Oxford and Cambridge. Academic and intellectual excellence became prized by prospective parents as much as social prestige among the benefits conferred by investment in the high fees of the independent schools. The cost seemed the more worthwhile with the abolition of many grammar schools, especially the direct grant grammar schools in 1975.[76] The well-to-do rode the inflation of fees with ease and the public schools continued to thrive. But what could be done to widen the social catchment downwards?

A serious attempt to do this was made with the Education Act 1980 which created the Assisted Places Scheme introduced in 1981.[77] This, an echo of Fleming and the Public Schools Commission, enables poorer children of high intelligence to attend fee paying schools at the taxpayers' expense. Some 229 schools participate including almost all the 119 direct grant grammar schools which had gone independent. Fifty-five thousand places are offered each year but only about 4,000 are taken up. The scheme meets opposition from those who consider the funds – £21m a year in 1985 – better spent in strengthening the maintained sector than in siphoning able children away from it. Yet for the children concerned it has brought benefits, with nearly 80 per cent of those who had passed through the system up to 1984 going on to higher education.[78]

The expansion of higher education, Robbins and after

In the inter-war years there had been little pressure on the universities or problem of selection. Virtually any student with the money and desire could go to university if he passed an easy matriculation examination. Demand for graduates was restricted and 'the pressure for degree courses was thus rather small and the capacity of the universities matched the demand'.[79] The vast potential demand from able people did not materialize because they could not contemplate the cost.

From the period immediately prior to the Second World War through to 1960 the university places about doubled:

Table 36: University students, 1938–9 and 1960–1

	Under-graduates	Advanced students	Total	First year students
1938–9	46,908	3,094	50,002	15,153
1960–1	89,863	17,836	107,699	29,510

Accordingly the chances of going to university increased appreciably for most classes.[80]

Table 37: Proportions of children from different social classes entering university, 1930s–1970s

	% of children born 1920–9 entering university 1938–47	% of children born late 1930s entering university mid 1950s	Halsey et al. % of 1972 sample[81]
Professional and managerial	6	14	20
Non-manual and skilled manual	1	2.5	–
Semi- and unskilled	0.5	0.5	1.8

Yet in the mid 1950s (1954–5) only 3.2 per cent of an age group overall went to university[82] or 3.8 per cent of boys and 1.5 per cent of girls.[83] Of Halsey's 1972 sample 5.1 per cent had been to university.

Behind these still small proportions in the 1950s lay evidence of clear wastage, as Furneaux found:[84]

Table 38: Wastage in university entrance, 1950s

of	10,607 11-year olds in primary schools in 1948	
	430 achieved two A levels mid 1950s	(4.05%)
of whom	394 applied to university	(3.71%)
of whom	281 were admitted	(2.64%)

This rejection of 28 per cent of candidates with two A levels suggested far too restricted a flow from sixth form to university. Even in 1964 before the expansion of the 1960s took effect 12 per cent of school leavers with respectable grades (two Bs or three Cs at A level) were rejected.[85] Furneaux presciently considered that intake levels to universities could beneficially be raised to 6.9 per cent of the age group.

Various factors made inevitable the subsequent expansion of the 1960s. First, there was an increasing 'trend' to staying on in the sixth form impelled by the desire for qualifications and made possible by the full employment and prosperous times of the 1950s. Boys and girls in sixth forms increased by 66 per cent from 32,000 to 53,000 between 1947 and 1958. Indeed 40 per cent of an age group of 14 in 1954 went into sixth forms as 17-year-olds in 1957.[86] Second, there was the problem of the birth 'bulge' of children born in the aftermath of the war who were due to come of age to enter the universities in the late 1960s. It was estimated that the population of 18-year-olds would rise from 533,000 in 1959 to a peak of 812,000 in 1965.[87] If no expansion of the universities occurred there would be a shortfall of 25,000 places for people qualified for and desiring university entrance but unable to find acceptance. Already in 1961 6.9 per cent of 18-year-olds had university entrance qualifications but only 4 per cent got into universities.[88] This situation was bound to deteriorate and Robbins called for an expansion of the universities to 197,000 by 1967–8.

Robbins further hoped that university expansion would rectify the imbalance between the social classes in their chances of university entrance. In 1958 children of the higher professional classes stood a 33 per cent chance of going to university: those of the semi- and unskilled only one per cent. Robbins could not believe that this wide spectrum truly represented the spread of ability between the social classes. Nor was it acceptable that the working classes should have steadily improved their chances of going to grammar school since before 1914 without this having any appreciable effect on their entry into higher education. Part of the problem in the 1950s was still lack of family finance among the lower classes. In a survey in the early 1950s it was found that 365 children from a sample of 1,473 grammar schools did not apply to universities for lack of family resources and 53 who won places had to decline them for the same reasons.[89] In 1962 grant changes abolished the competitive state and LEA scholarship system and placed on LEAs the obligation to finance any qualified student who gained a university place. It was hoped that the removal of financial barriers would encourage the flow upwards from the lower classes to higher education.

The introduction of comprehensives was also thought to have improved the flow of potential talent to the universities. In 1968 13 per cent of comprehensive pupils entering university had actually failed the 11+. In fact enough 11+ 'failures' were getting to university in the late 1960s to fill a university the size of Leicester every year.[90] One of the best studies of an individual school confirms this. Creighton School in Harringey raised its university entrance rate to over 40 a year compared with the 14–16 achieved by the schools from which Creighton had been formed.[91]

Fuelled by these and other considerations[92] university places almost doubled:

Table 39: University students, 1960–1 and 1967–8

	1960–1	1967–8
undergraduates	89,863	164,653
postgraduates	17,836	35,019
all students	107,699	200,121

This raised the proportion of an age group going to university to a modest 6.3 per cent.[93]

The present flow of students into higher education is as follows:

Table 40: Students in higher education, 1979–85

	Full time[94] university students	Polytechnic[95] students	All[96] higher education	Age participation[97] ratio of university entrants
1979	249,500	199,500	510,000	7.6
1980	254,200	202,100	521,000	7.6
1981	255,200	213,600	542,000	7.4
1982	250,600	220,800	553,000	6.9
1983	246,900	231,900	566,000	6.6
1984	245,000	237,800	573,000	
1985			579,000	

The expansion of higher education as a whole in recent years is something of which the Conservative government is rightly proud. But it has been brought about by beginning the contraction of the universities and expanding the lower cost alternative of the polytechnics and colleges of higher education. Entry to universities in spite of the Robbins expansion still remains restricted to a relatively small élite.

IV

From the 'ladder' to the 'pool':
the concepts behind the system

So far we have been concerned with the evolution of policy. But underlying these policies and their changes were certain abstract concepts. They could be held at one level as high philosophical and theological beliefs, at another as half-baked public attitudes whose acceptance made policies practicable. They ranged from strong visual images like the 'ladder of opportunity' to highly ambiguous concepts like 'equality'. Some regarded equality as incompatible with notions of freedom and justice. Others linked it with the older phraseology of the 1930s and 1940s ideal of 'equality of opportunity'. Beliefs in 'intelligence', the 'pool of ability', or their denial, were also implicit assumptions in the minds of those seeking to effect or resist policy changes. Because they were often used in slogans to influence opinion, the words expressing these concepts were regarded as clearer and firmer in content than they could be. Their ambiguities and implications were usually left unexplored by those who repeated the clichés lightly. It is the purpose of this section to examine some of these notions, the mental baggage of those shaping the system.

The 'ladder of opportunity'

The first concept which broke down the assumption that elementary and secondary education should relate to different social classes was that of the ladder of opportunity. This envisaged by its narrow imagery, a difficult steep climbing relationship whereby a few very able children clambered in small numbers from one level to another. It was possible but arduously difficult. The use of the imagery of ladders dates back at least to the 1870s. T. H. Huxley addressing the London School Board called for 'a great educational ladder, the bottom of which should be in the gutter and the top in the University and by which every child who had the strength to climb might, by using that strength, reach the place intended for him'.[1] Viscount Bryce's Commission on Secondary Education in 1895 was concerned that the higher professions should be replenished by talent from different sources and not become the preserve of any self-perpetuating order. Accordingly it welcomed the expansion of scholarships as 'indispensable steps in that educational ladder by means of which boys of rare capacity may pass from elementary schools to the universities'. The beneficiaries, in his famous phrase, should be 'candidates of exceptional rather than average ability'.[2] Opponents of this kind of mobility, on the contrary, could talk of the dangers of 'forcing up' children 'into a totally different stratum' on the analogy of water or oil pumps.[3] They also spoke of 'overpressure', another image-laden term used to criticize the pumping of education into the brains of groups not deemed fitting to receive it. The 'ladder' image became very common in the 1900s enabling critics of the education system to refer vividly to missing rungs or the lack of a firm footing.

It was Sydney Webb who was particularly fond of using this image. As Chairman of the London Technical Education Board he had created a network of scholarships enabling able children to move up through various levels of institutions – a 'capacity-catching machine'. His 2000 scholarships provided children of London wage earners with 'a genuinely accessible ladder'.[4] Lord Haldane, whose interests were chiefly in higher education, also used the imagery. Lord Ashby notes that 'he [Haldane] returned repeatedly in his speeches to the concept of a unified, articulated state system of education, a ladder from primary school to university with no rungs missing'.[5]

The notion of the ladder was an advance on earlier assumptions that working class children could have no access to secondary education. Yet the narrowness of the ladder as an object reflected the narrowness of the system of which it was an image. It had strong Social Darwinist overtones of upward struggle – 'the upward path' was another Bryce image – with only the fittest reaching the top. As Webb was the first to admit, it could not suggest education for all: 'construct what scholarship ladder we will, the secondary school can only be used by a small fraction of the population'.[6] He had a vision of something wider: 'the democratic ideal in education is not merely that a ladder should be provided whereby a few students may climb unimpeded . . . What the national well-being demands . . . is that *every* child . . . should receive *all* the education requisite for the full development of its faculties.'[7]

Accordingly many who looked forward to an educational system allowing a wider access preferred to abandon the image of the ladder in favour of something broader. J. A. Hobson called for:

> not an educational ladder, narrowing as it rises, to be climbed with difficulty by a chosen energetic few, who, as they rise, enter a new social stratum . . . It is a broad, easy stair, and not a narrow ladder, that is wanted, one which will entice everyone to rise, will make for general and not for selected culture.[8]

Another new image representing the movement of children in the system was the sieve. Sir Martin Conway, Conservative MP for the Combined English Universities, elaborated this:

> It is not, in fact, a ladder that we want from the lowest slum to the highest university honour, what we want is a sieve, so that we may be quite sure that not a grain is kept above the sieve that can get through it, and that not a grain large enough to remain in the top of the sieve gets lost. We want to sift the millions of children born in this country to discover, to isolate, to bring out, to help in every way, all the finest ability in the country, and allow none of it to escape.[9]

The shift from the ladder or the staircase to the sieve was quite a subtle one. The former implied individuals propelling themselves upwards – or not – according to their own volition and ability. The sieve implied some external agency, the state, positively separating and lifting irrespective of the will of the individual 'grains' in the sieve. The ladder emphasized the benefits to the individual; the sieve those to the state. In terms of the realities of politics the ladder and stair predominated before 1944; the sieve with the virtually universal sitting of the 11+ after 1944. But neither the ladder nor the sieve implied equality.

The concept of equality

Those who wished to get away from the Edwardian ladder view stressed the rights of children to secondary education for all based on notions of equality. Yet 'equality' was to become the most widely interpreted term in educational discussion, meaning quite different things to different people. At the most profound level it had theological roots. Archbishop Temple, an important influence on the 1944 Act, reminded his readers, 'if all are children of one Father, then all are equal heirs of a status in comparison with which the apparent differences of quality and capacity are unimportant; in the deepest and most important of all – their relationship to God – all are equal.'[10] For Temple it was inconsistent with this that some children should be given the educational opportunities to develop their capacities and others not. Christian theorists of educational equality shared and emphasized this view. R. H. Tawney, the author of *Equality* (1931), was the leading Socialist exponent of secondary education for all and equality of opportunity. One of the pillars of his position was the Christian concept of common humanity. Tawney and Temple were close throughout their lives, meeting at Rugby, both Fellows of Balliol, leaders of the WEA and active in Anglican movements for social awareness and reform. Tawney certainly read the draft of and influenced Temple's *Christianity and Social Order* which in turn influenced the 1944 Education Act.[11] If Christianity was at the root of left-wing theories of equality in education so it was for the Minister of Education, Lord Eccles, on the Right. For him it was 'the triumph of Christianity to have implanted this idea [the equality of common humanity] so firmly'.[12] Yet descending from this high moral–theological plane the relationship of equality to education in practice could lead to very varied interpretations.

It should be made clear at the outset that what advocates of equality in education did *not* believe was that children or adults were perfectly equal in mental capacities and natural abilities. It is a crude and easy argument of anti-egalitarians that their opponents do hold this view. In practice such a standpoint would be so absurd that I have encountered nobody in this debate who seeks to sustain it. Tawney put this clearly:

The equality which all these thinkers emphasize as desirable is not equality of capacity or attainment, but of circumstances and institutions and the manner of life. The inequality which they deplore is not inequality of personal gifts, but of the social and economic environment.[13]

Accordingly, 'to criticize inequality and to desire equality is not, as is sometimes suggested, to cherish the romantic illusion that men are equal in character and intelligence'.[14] It was equally romantic and inconceivable that education should lead to identical lifestyles and living standards for all.

Equality in educational terms did not imply the suggestion that all abilities were equal or that all outcomes should be the same but there should be greater 'equality of opportunity'. Haldane was one of the earliest to use the term 'equality of educational opportunity' frequently in his speeches. 'Until we have given democracy that equality of educational opportunity, the democracy will always be restless.' Yet as a 'ladder' man he did not yet believe it to be practical: 'you cannot in practice give complete equality in educational opportunity to all classes' because only a few could step up the ladder.[15]

In the inter-war years those who wished to move towards an educational system based not on the ladder but on 'secondary education for all' believed in the genuine possibilities of 'equality of opportunity'. This was the thrust of R. H. Tawney's influential lectures of 1929. In his view communities needed to draw on streams of fresh talent to nourish their higher ranks. Otherwise they were in danger of stagnating if they were perpetually drawn from narrow social and economic origins. Moreover, 'unless individuals of ability can turn their powers to account they are embittered by a sense of defeat and frustration'.[16] For the health of all levels of society, for the curbing of arrogance at the top and the alleviating of resentment at the bottom, greater possibilities for equality were desirable. Several strategies could help to bring this about – redistributive and progressive taxation, trade union power to raise wages, the extension of the social services. But a key strategy was the reduction of inequality through the extension of educational opportunities. A political opponent of Tawney's, the Conservative president of the Board of Education, Eustace Percy, agreed that 'the demand for real "equality of opportunity" in education was becoming nothing less than the main popular motive for political action.'[17]

If the phrase was in common use in the inter-war years, it became a recurrent cliché in the 1940s, especially in the thinking behind the 1944 Education Act. The possibility of reform forced people to think of the different meanings behind the concept. Was it to mean that all children would receive the same secondary education? Or were they to receive an education equal to their abilities? Or was the equality that of the opportunity to take the same selection examination? Equality could refer to the relationship beween one child and other, or that between a child's ability and the school to which he was allotted, or to the equality of all children before the judgement of the selecting and differentiating 11+ examination. Most people probably did not think too clearly about the implications of this but those who hoped for a switch to the multilateral comprehensive clearly had broader expectations of equality than those who wished to advance by extending the opportunities for grammar school attendance.

The Green Book discussion document of 1941, shaping opinion for the 1944 Act, addressed the issue directly:[18]

'Equality of opportunity' does not mean that all children should receive the same form of education. At the primary stage i.e., to the age of 11, education should be the same for all, but thereafter at the secondary stage there must be ample variety of educational opportunity to meet the very varying requirements and capacities of the children. Indeed, in the educational sphere, much more than in the dietetic, one child's meat may be another child's poison. The provision for all children at the secondary stage of the same type of education would not connote equality of opportunity but rather the reverse, as it would involve large numbers of children receiving an education that could not possibly fulfil the purposes indicated in the opening paragraph. Equality of opportunity means, therefore, acceptance of the principle that the accidents of parental circumstances or place of residence shall not preclude any child from receiving the education from which he is best capable of profiting.

It will be clear from what has been said that by 'secondary education for all' is meant not the provision of the same type of education for all at the secondary stage, but that all types of full-time education at this stage should be regarded as on a parity and should receive equal treatment in such matters as accommodation, staffing, size of classes, etc.

The 1944 Act accordingly embodied equality in different senses. There was the equality of opportunity of all primary children to take the same 11+ examination which would then indicate how unequal in attainments they were. There was also the genuine belief that an equality was achieved between a child's mental abilities and the school to which he was allocated. More tenuously it was suggested that the different types of schools, grammar and secondary modern, were really equal in that they should enjoy 'parity of esteem' – Norwood's phrase rather than Butler's. Ronald Gould of the NUT had called in 1943 for 'equal opportunities in schools of equal social standing giving courses of equal duration under equivalent conditions'.[19] But this was not to be. The equality of 1944 embodied a greater concern for diversity of abilities and outcomes than for such uniformity.

As high hopes for the outcome of the 1944 Act waned so there was more questioning of the equality concept it enshrined. Mary Warnock pinpointed the attitudes implicit in the implementation of the 1944 Act:

> The equality of opportunity offered by the Act was the opportunity, now open to children to *compete for* the best education for which they could be selected . . . [the] theory underlying the introduction of the 11+ test was that if a child did not win the best in the competition, he did at any rate win what was best for *him*, since he was *ex hypothesi* not a winner so the prize would not in any case have been suitable for him . . . The argument seemed to be that if you did not win a grammar school place then you had not really needed it.[20]

Thus, under this 'weak' notion of equality, children were seen to have equality of opportunity to compete for a place in an élitist system which left people unequal. Accordingly some theorists wanted to move to a 'strong' concept of equality which engineered not merely opportunities but an egalitarian outcome. As A. H. Halsey argued, what was needed in the 1970s was not only 'equality of access' but 'equality of outcome'.[21] Anthony Crosland, the chief theoretician of the Labour Party, emphasized this view in the mid-1970s. Socialism for him was basically about equality, but 'by equality we meant more than a meritocratic society of equal opportunities in which the greatest rewards would go to those with the most fortunate genetic endowment and family background.'[22]

This was merely the 'liberal' or 'weak' definition. 'We wanted a wider social equality . . . indeed all that was enshrined in the age old socialist dream of a more classless society.' For the Left the mechanism now was to be the comprehensive school and the abolition of the grammar school which Crosland urged on. Equality of opportunity expressed through the 11+ and tripartite system had been too subject to the inequalities of home background and social factors which in turn had produced further inequalities in their outcome. A shift to a more radical 'strong' form of equality *pur sang* would entail the abolition of public schools, grammar schools and the assurance not only of secondary education for all but a common comprehensive education for all. Such an outright espousal would bring equality into a clash with 'equality of opportunity' itself.

Sir Keith Joseph as the leading theoretician of the Right and Secretary of State for Education seized on this paradox in the late 1970s. He approved of equality of opportunity as an attack on privilege in the name of liberty. Yet he emphasized that 'equality of results is itself the enemy of equality of opportunity'.[23] Equality of opportunity implied the removal of external barriers preventing the individual from exploiting his talents. Yet since all individuals have totally disparate talents and levels of ability the freedom to develop them must lead to commensurately diverse and unequal outcomes. Inequality was the inevitable result of the free and equal opportunity of unequals to exercise unequal abilities. As Joseph's Cabinet colleague Lord Hailsham had earlier put it,[24] if there is equality of educational opportunity there must be inequality of reward for those who persevere and pass examinations compared with those who do not. Moreover it has been suggested by Douglas and others that true equality of opportunity is vitiated by varieties of encouraging or stultifying home backgrounds. In that case even the equalization of opportunities could only be achieved by equalizing living standards and an unimaginable interference with the relationships of children, homes and parents. Thus not only was equality of outcome incompatible with equality of opportunity but the social engineering of both would entail an unacceptable interference with the liberty of the individual. Equality stands in confrontation with its uneasy neighbours 'liberty' and 'justice'.

Reservations about the desirability of overall equality were also raised by the influential work of John Rawls on the theory of justice – one element in Sir Keith Joseph's thought. Rawls' view was that the democratic concept of liberty combines both fair equality of opportunity and the difference principle. Ideally social and economic inequalities are acceptable if equality of opportunity and the inequalities of outcome result in benefits to the most advantaged which also benefit the least. As Rawls put it, 'Those who have been favoured by nature, whoever they are, may gain from their good fortune only on terms that improve the situation of those who have lost out.'[25] One cannot and should not eliminate distinctions of natural ability and privileged education but 'the basic structure can be arranged so that these contingencies work for the good of the least fortunate.' We can see the pragmatic strength of this argument in the English case. Prince Charles, for example, has enjoyed the unusual privilege of access to education at Gordonstoun, Geelong and Trinity College Cambridge which have contributed to shape his manifestly high qualities of mind and character. Yet that Prince Charles possesses such qualities as a Prince and future King benefits all Englishmen as his subjects, probably even more than it does him himself. In the same way patients benefit from a well-educated surgeon, employees and shareholders from a well-educated company chairman, soldiers from well-educated senior officers and so forth. There is no case for equalizing down the education of princes, surgeons and generals. The unequal excellence of their education conveys benefits to those beneath them which would not be maximized if all educational experiences were equalized.

Nowhere was the conceptual clash between freedom and equality more evident than in attitudes to the public schools. Tawney, himself a product of Rugby, had attacked the public schools fiercely in *Equality*.[26] The majority of people could not attend them, they were socially divisive, coarsened intellectual and spiritual standards, restricted the sources of leadership and succeeded in 'pampering one class' and 'depressing another'. Yet Tawney did not propose the forcible suppression of the public schools for all their undermining of equality. He hoped that the state system would so improve as to leave the independent schools as a 'minor category' within the system. Thus even Tawney was not prepared for Equality to override Liberty in the abolition of the public schools. The other leading theoretician of the Left, Anthony

Crosland, felt equally strongly about the 'glaring injustice' of the public schools. But he too demurred at abolition. More explicitly than Tawney he faced the equality–freedom issue: 'a flat proscription is undesirable on libertarian grounds . . . the interference with private liberty would be intolerable.'[27] When Crosland became responsible for education in the 1960s he retained this view in spite of increasing pressures from the Labour Party for the total abolition of the public schools.[28] Defenders of the public schools within the Conservative Party and the independent sector itself likewise stressed the priority of freedom over equality. Timothy Raison put it squarely: 'any attempt to abolish the independent schools . . . would represent an utterly unacceptable attack on the principles of freedom and the plural society.'[29] In practice, freedom would always defeat equality over this issue. It would be dangerously undemocratic to forbid people to found schools. In any case, parents denied access to public schools in Britain could easily send their offspring on a short journey to public schools which would surely emerge offshore or in Ireland or the Continent. The more practical path to equality for Tawney and Crosland was not to degrade or abolish superior independent education. It was to equalize the attractiveness of independent and state education by raising the quality of the latter. Quality and Equality would not be incompatible enemies. On the contrary improved quality in the state secondary schools would be the path to egalitarianism in an even balance of state and independent sectors. Such was the ideal.

If equality clashed with liberty especially over the rights of parents to opt for independent education so it could clash with the concept of justice.[30] David Eccles when Minister of Education observed: 'you have got to choose beween justice and equality because you cannot have both principles at once. Those who support the comprehensive school prefer equality. Her Majesty's Government prefer justice.' It could be argued that able talent deserved to be cultivated in schools appropriate to its ability. To educate academically able children along with those of ordinary average intelligence would be to hold back the former and prevent their fullest development. This might achieve equality of treatment for the mass at the expense of grossest injustice to the able individual. This view has been expressed across a wide spectrum of opinion. The Socialist Sir Ronald Gould, Secretary of the NUT, deplored levelling down and the confusion of equality and equality of opportunity. For him it would be a travesty to achieve equality in education by teaching all children in the same way, 'for it hampers human development and denies human rights. The hare has rights as well as the tortoise.'[31] This denial of rights in the name of equality would be an injustice.

The injustice of egalitarian education has been most strongly emphasized by some of the Black Paper contributors.[32] They attacked egalitarians for disliking 'any process which enables some children to emerge markedly ahead of their fellows'. The campaign for equality, in their view, has been less concerned with raising opportunities for the lowest than with holding back the best and 'levelling down the higher standards towards a uniform mediocrity'. The egalitarians are seen not as wanting to bring all to an equal starting line but of seeing education as a handicap race in which some must be held back – in this they would agree with Gould's comments about the rights of the hare. Indeed to deliberately oblige children to receive an education worse than they could potentially receive and benefit from is itself a grave injustice. As an experienced headmaster observed, 'the greatest inequality of the present age is the equal treatment of unequals.'[33] Here was a subtle form of egalitarian injustice. Paradoxically, the injustice of Victorian times was the totally unequal and different forms of education given to children of the same ability but born into widely different social classes. The 1870s' unequal treatment of equals was as unjust as the 1970s' equal treatment of unequals, in their view. Anti-egalitarians would regard English education as having swung from one form of injustice to another. They would see the just equilibrium in this arc as the late 1940s and 1950s, the justice secured by the mechanisms of the 11+ and the grammar school.

The meritocracy

A belief in equality of opportunity did not necessarily entail a rejection of élitism. Indeed quite the contrary, since one of the motives of early espousers of the concept was the very need to refresh the élite from below by talent from different social classes. The whole mechanism of the 11+ and the tripartite system was designed to produce an academic élite, more fairly based indeed than before 1944, but an élite none the less. Crosland was candid: 'Now some degree of éliteness is inevitable in any society – and indeed desirable for we are not trying to create a mediocre mass society, in which everyone is levelled down to a uniform denominator.'[34] These were appropriate views for an ex-public school man and Oxford don. Indeed the notion of a society without some kind of élite is well nigh unimaginable. Yet an élite based on personal ability, selected by a fair educational system was regarded as preferable to one perpetuating itself either by the prescriptive right of its social origins or by a public school and university education purchased by money rather than earned by merit. This is what egalitarians like Crosland and Tawney wanted, not the mediocre levelling down which anti-egalitarians claimed to fear. Such a new élite was termed a 'meritocracy' by Michael Young, who was a close personal friend and mentor of Crosland. But around this concept clustered further problems.

Many hoped that the possibility of perfect 'equality of opportunity', with talent flowing up in a smooth capillary action through the education system, would lead to the creation of a meritocracy.[35] Such a society would not be equal in its consequences but a new meritocratic élite based on examination-selected intelligence and achievement would replace that of birth and inherited wealth. This change was not viewed as an unmixed blessing.

One consequence of the rise of a meritocracy would be the creation of a genuinely inferior class at the bottom of society. The Victorian labourer whatever his poverty and sense of social inferiority always enjoyed a psychological comfort. He knew, or could believe, that his station in life was not due to any failing on his part but to the structure within which he was placed. He lacked access to secondary education and the examinations through which he could have advanced himself. Yet his fellows were all in the same boat; there was no need for jealousy of them or recrimination about himself. The late twentieth century unskilled or unemployed labourer, after all the educational reforms, is in a psychologically much more vulnerable situation. He is at the end of a long sequence of failing every examination and neglecting every opportunity placed before him. He is confronted with the fact that his fault lies in himself. As Young notes: 'For the first time in human history the inferior man has no ready buttress for his self-regard.' Some indeed see meritocracy as but a new kind of social democratic right-wing society 'where the people at the bottom will no longer have the consolation of knowing that they are there by accident rather than examination'.[36] The dangerous feelings of lack of self worth if not self-loathing that can result from this cruel confrontation already manifest themselves in too many familiar forms of deviant behaviour, the violence, football and other hooliganism and vandalism which are among the nastier aspects of British life.

A second disadvantage arising from meritocratic mobility and equality of opportunity is the effect not only on the failures but on some of the successes. Richard Hoggart has written sensitively of the problems of the scholarship boy:

> Almost every working class [scholarship winning] boy finds himself chafing against his environment during adolescence. He is at the friction point of two cultures . . . He is in a way cut off by his parents as much as by his talent which urges him to break away from his group . . . He has to be more and more alone.[37]

Willy Russell's 'Rita' put it more directly:

> *Rita:* But studyin' was just for wimps, wasn't it? See if I'd started takin' school seriously I would have had to become different from me mates, an' that's not allowed.
> *Frank:* By whom?
> *Rita:* By your mates, by your family, by everyone.[38]

Meritocracy entailed its strains for the successful – and would-be successful like Rita – as for the failures. Yet their problems are probably less important than the potentially harmful consequences of meritocracy for political and industrial life.

For, thirdly, meritocracy creams off talent from areas where it is needed in the lower ranks of society. It is argued that before the 1940s the trade union and labour movement benefited greatly from men of high intelligence and genuinely working class background. They stayed within their own class to work for its benefit in union or political fields. The obvious cases are men like Ernest Bevin, George Tomlinson, Aneurin Bevan who in later circumstances might have risen through scholarships, grammar schools and Oxbridge to lucrative careers in the professions or business. Were all its most able men creamed off by the education system and decanted into the professional middle classes the Labour movement both industrial and political would be left seriously debilitated. In practice this has not truly come about as working class men and women with higher education have percolated back into Labour politics.

If the debilitation of the Labour movement by efficient educational mobility has proved an ungrounded fear, a more serious one has been the haemorrhaging of talent from the craftsmen and foreman classes. The superb quality of so much Victorian and Edwardian craftsmanship was the product of trapped talent, of intelligent men not permitted by the education system to move away from manual work. The careful intelligence behind the silversmithing, tailoring, housebuilding and decorating of the 1890s and 1900s would in later generations be applied to book learning. The loss is certain, the gain more problematic.

Fourthly, the exact deployment of individuals to positions in society and to occupations precisely matching their educational and intellectual attainments could have a chilling effect. The inhabitants of Aldous Huxley's *Brave New World* were so graduated:[39]

> Alpha children wear grey. They work much harder than we do, because they're so frightfully clever. I'm really awfully glad I'm a Beta because I don't work so hard. And then we are much better than the Gammas and Deltas. Gammas are stupid . . . and Epsilons are still worse. They're too stupid to be able to read or write.

An Alpha may be Director of Hatcheries and Conditioning, an Epsilon-Minus Semi-Moron (simian, dwarf-like and dressed in black) is a lift attendant. Yet in Huxley's scenario Alphas and Epsilons were genetically engineered to be so from the embryo, not sieved and selected through competitive education for their positions.

Finally, in the debate on equality, there were those who saw some conflict between the meritocracy and the wider national culture. T. S. Eliot was perhaps their leading spokesman.[40] As he told G. H. Bantock 'You can have equality; you can have culture, but you cannot have both.' He deplored 'the headlong rush to educate everyone' resulting from the 1944 Act, disapproved of a society ruled by persons who had passed examinations and regarded 'the ideal of an educational system which would auto-matically sort out everyone according to his native capacities' as 'unattainable in practice'. He regarded with distaste the increase of higher education as leading to a 'lowering of standards' – this in 1948 when barely three per cent of young people went to university in England! Eliot's chief fear was that education created élites which were not the same as an upper class. For him it was necessary that there be a continuity of leading families who embody an accumula-tion of social and cultural wisdom which they transmit through their stability. Élites rise and fall according to their intelligence which will vary from generation to generation and the educational opportunities available to them. As Bantock notes, 'a society based on meritocracy implies a too great mobility', and for Eliot it lacks the tradition for the transmission of culture. A society needs its turnover of meritocratic élites but not at the expense of its culture-transmitting and longer lasting higher classes.

It is worth pausing here to recapitulate and clarify some important distinctions. Equality is not the same as equality of opportunity. Moreover the advocates of either or both of these concepts are not always clear at what point they would wish them to apply. Most would agree that individuals are equal under God or the law and yet likewise agree that they are all unequal in terms of natural aptitudes and capabilities. The recognition of equality in one area is quite compatible with recognition of their inequalities in another. Yet these unequal natural capabilities are to be offered educational opportunities so the next issue is whether these should be equal or unequal. To have the opportunity of doing something is not the same as being able to do it. Yet just as surely *not* to have the opportunity of doing something *is* the same as *not* being able to do it. Some would argue that to offer a superior education to those with already superior natural abilities is to compound the unfair inequality of nature with that of human institutions. Others would hold that to offer the same equal education to children of unequal levels of ability is to treat the able unfairly and unequally. This could be seen as the 'unfair' counterpart of counteracting the disadvantages of the dull child by buying for him a superior private education. Parallel to the inequalities of the education received by children are the inequalities of home background which have a powerful interrelationship with their education. But whatever can be done to equalize education by institutional reform, the home remains inviolate from such interference. Beyond school and home lie the inequalities of outcome. However equalized the institutions of education may become, yet the inequalities of ability and home will always lead to a spectrum of unequal outcomes of relative success and failure. Indeed this is necessary to create the occupants of the wide range of intellectual and menial tasks society requires. Aldous Huxley in his *Brave New World* imagined Cyprus entirely colonized by Alphas. Since none would undertake lower than Alpha jobs society collapsed and most of the new colonialists killed each other off in civil war. We should remember that there are many forms of equality and inequality. Some are inevitable and some highly desirable. Yet others are neither, and some of these are the product of human choice and equally amenable to human change.

Intelligence and the pool of ability

Perhaps the most important concept underlying this whole issue was that of 'intelligence'. The word had long meant 'knowledge' or 'information' and evolutionists such as Spencer and Galton had begun to slant its meaning towards the modern usage. But in the 1900s at a time of rapid advance in many areas of psychology it came to acquire its twentieth-century sense of innate reasoning and understanding ability. In France in 1905 Alfred Binet devised his first intelligence tests and scale, working out from large samples of Parisian schoolchildren what were normal mental capacities for each age. In 1911 the German William Stern devised his Intelligence Quotient (IQ) on the basis of this. Cyril Burt, the psychologist of the LCC, wrote his first study on experimental tests of general intelligence in 1909 and wrote extensively on the Binet scale in the years 1913–15.[41] Educational psychometrics and the concept of measurable intelligence thus arrived quite rapidly in England in the early years of this century.

An early use of intelligence testing had been as a yardstick for measuring mentally defective children. But in the inter-war years the concept of intelligence and its testing came to be used for 11+ selection to the grammar school. It was fortuitous that the rapid rise of interest in intelligence measurement from 1905 coincided with the 1907 Regulations for transferring children from elementary schools to forms of secondary education. Morant had not envisaged any connection between the two developments. But in the inter-war years 11+ testing and intelligence testing came to be closely associated. Between 1944 and the advent of the comprehensive school they were inseparable.

In 1919 Bradford started using Burt's intelligence tests in the scholarship examinations. Then from 1925 Godfrey Thomson at Edinburgh began to develop the Moray House tests which came to be commonly adopted by LEAs. Between 1925 and 1940 38 LEAs used the Moray House tests and 49 did not. As these intelligence tests came to be quite widely used even before 1944 so the belief in the concept of intelligence was yet more widespread and entrenched. But did it exist?

Cyril Burt, Professor of Psychology at London University, was the most influential advocate of the notion of intelligence as 'innate, general, cognitive ability'. In his belief it was inborn and the product of genetic, hereditary factors. Moreover he held that an individual's IQ, received at birth, remained approximately constant throughout his life. Intelligence itself increased through childhood into early adulthood but IQ measured mental age. This remains roughly constant and accordingly it was as valid to test it at 10 as at any other age. Third, he believed in an approximately normal distribution of intelligence over the population as a whole. Whole populations could not improve their average or the normal distribution curve of their intelligence any more than individuals could do so through changes in their environment.

These characteristics of intelligence, confirmed in the public mind by the authority of the doyen of the field were in accord with contemporary institutions. Intelligent professional parents were reassured that their offspring were likely to inherit their intelligence and accordingly their right to places in academic grammar schools as fee payers. Nor was it surprising that the lower orders doing less intelligent jobs should produce children very few of whom could have inherited sufficient intelligence to merit academic secondary education. Furthermore the belief that IQ remained constant throughout life justified testing it at 10 as well as at any other age. The idea also that intelligence could be measured as a constant normal distribution justified the setting of normative proportions of grammar school entrants coming from the elementary schools. This view of intelligence was 'one of the main stumbling blocks in the way of egalitarian sympathies'.[42] In particular, advocates of the comprehensive school attacked the intelligence test, 11+ selection and the tripartite divisions of secondary education all of which the comprehensive school would obviate. At the end of his life Burt contributed to the Black Papers, knowingly, and tragically, using material now known to be quite fraudulent to 'prove' a decline in educational standards. It was sad that Burt who had started his career sympathetically studying poor, backward and delinquent children and whose knighthood had been conferred by Attlee's Labour government ended his life being regarded as a deranged educational reactionary.

Burt, however, had nothing to do with the pseudo-scientific views of intelligence expressed by the Norwood Committee that it could be neatly divided into abstract, mechanical and concrete. Neither Burt nor any other psychologist was consulted on these deliberations which were based on pragmatic observation. It was remarkable that these three clear types of intelligence discerned by the Committee just happened to relate exactly to the grammar, technical and modern school divisions already long in existence. It provided a rough and ready psychological justification for not changing existing administrative structures and the social class attitudes they embodied. The concept of intelligence which had started as a scientific statistical exercise had become highly politicized. Seemingly used by the Right to defend the status quo of a divisive system it was regarded by the Left as a bogus barrier to genuine equality of opportunity.

The concept of intelligence, its measurability and normal distribution lay behind another major concept, that of the 'pool of ability'. The suggested proportions of working class children in grammar school intakes (Sir Robert Morant's 25 per cent in the 1900s and Sir Charles Trevelyan's 40 per cent in the 1920s), the norm that 20 per cent of the population should receive a grammar school education, the cool acceptance of less than 5 per cent of an age group's receiving a university education and of 75 per cent being regarded as 11+ failures – all these set or accepted norms assumed a limited pool of ability. Only a limited number of young people were capable of benefiting from anything more than the basic forms of education provided for all. At the most obvious level there will always be differences 'between a Newton or a Leonardo and Poor Tom the Fool' as Lord Robbins put it. [43] But for the 90 per cent (or more) of children who are neither born geniuses nor idiots it is difficult to define the percentage which might be capable of any particular level. It is even more difficult to defend the indefinite retention of the levels laid down at some particular historical stage – the 1910s, 1930s or even 1950s.

Accordingly in the 1960s the notion of the pool came to be questioned. In particular it was evident that the size of any pool was not fixed but could be increased or diminished by external factors. Sir John Newsom noted that 'intellectual talent is not a fixed quantity . . . but a variable that can be modified by social policy and educational approaches'. [44] In particular as schools improved in quality and parents became more appreciative of the importance of education so 'the pool itself becomes wider and deeper increasing the numbers of very able children'. [45] In Stephen Wiseman's view even slight improvements in the quality of teachers would affect the size of the pool they produced: 'there is an enormous reservoir of ability waiting to be tapped'. Robbins likewise could not believe that the pool of ability in the semi- and unskilled working class was limited to the one per cent who struggled to university before his Report. Rising living standards, home backgrounds and the proportion within the middle class who themselves had experienced more education would affect the size of the pool:

> The numbers who are capable of benefiting from higher education are a function not only of heredity but also of a host of other influences varying with standards of educational provision, family incomes and attitudes and the education received by previous generations. If there is to be talk of a pool of ability, it must be a pool which surpasses the widow's cruse in the Old Testament in that when more is taken for higher education in one generation more will tend to be available in the next. [46]

The belief in a small pool of ability and in the need to keep this pool small in order to maintain high standards can lead to some odd conclusions. It would be possible to have a system in which the quality of graduates was preserved by creaming off ten per cent of primary school children to grammar schools and allowing into higher education only those who could win open scholarships to Oxford and Cambridge. Then only those who obtained 'firsts' could be awarded degrees. The quality of the output would be superb and the standards as high as anyone could wish. Science graduates would be as rare as FRSs. Yet in the real world – where, for example, GEC alone recruits 1,500 graduates a year and complains of the shortage – this is nonsense.[47] British industry and all the other services of the nation do not run on a few Oxbridge 'firsts' but on thousands of 'seconds' from Loughborough and Hull and a couple of score of similar valuable institutions. The problem is that the visual image of the pool suggests a clear distinction between a small number in the pool and a vast majority out of it. In reality things are a finely shaded continuum. The edge of the pool is not the hard tiled edge of the swimming bath but a very marshy water margin.

The danger of thinking in terms of the pool is that it leads to a focusing on the best to the neglect of the good. English education has always excelled in fostering high abilities at the top end of the system. It is relatively easy to do and academics prefer working with well selected students. Yet too often this has entailed a neglect and even denigration of the much more difficult problem of the education of the second and third rate on the edge of the pool. Too much attention to producing graduates and too little to apprentice technicians? Too much prestige for the grammar school and too little for the Junior Technical School? These are familiar and historical issues that underlie some of Britain's problems. Achieving excellence through restrictive pools regardless of the wider needs of society has little value in itself other than to delight dons. The good can be the enemy of the excellent but the excellent can also be the enemy of the competent and we have need of them all.

The recognition of the need for wide ranges of ability came to be expressed in the concept of the stock of human capital. In the 1950s economists were increasingly aware of the importance of education for economic growth.[48] This became more formally expressed in 1961 by T. W. Schultz as 'human capital'.[49] It was pointed out that increases in national output could not entirely be explained in terms of growth of the traditional factors of production – land, labour and capital. In Schultz's view 'involvement in human capital is probably the major explanation for this difference . . . such investment in human capital accounts for most of the impressive rise in the real earnings per worker.' This human capital was the increased quality of labour reflecting itself in effort. The enhanced quality itself arose from the discipline, skill, training, knowledge of the labour force inculcated by education.[50] Indeed education and this human capital which it created came to be regarded as 'residual' factors in economic growth, these non-material and not easily measurable qualitative factors which in modern societies play an indisputable role in growth.

One of the problems with the concept however was how far education was an investment in human capital and how far merely a consumption good to be enjoyed by the recipient. The study of poetry or art history or philosophy may give satisfaction to the student. Yet such studies have less justifiable value as investment in economic growth than, more obviously, engineering or computing studies. Arthur Lewis makes three useful distinctions. There is consumption education to be enjoyed by the student as is any other consumer service like travel or going to the theatre. Second, there is productive investment education, often scientific and technological and leading directly to increased economic production. Third, social investment education may lead indirectly to production by inculcating attitudes such as receptivity to ideas, social discipline, aptitude for operating in a factory or urban organization and so forth. In practice there may be much overlap between these divisions. They all add to that stock of human capital of skills, aptitudes and attitudes which is as important as the more obviously tangible financial and material factors of production.

Since the 1900s it is clear that there has been a tendency to think of the flow of people through the education system in terms of visual concepts. Notions of ladders, broad staircases, sieves, equalizing starting posts, pools and stock succeed each other as the clichés and platitudes of the day. Overall the changing images represent a broad shift. In the early century the 'ladder' emphasized education as a privilege made available to a select few for their own advantage and advancement. In later years the 'pool' and the 'stock of capital' emphasize the need of the state and society for mass quantities of ability at all levels for the common prosperity and well being.

V

The Conditions of Progress

The evolution of educational policy was underlain not only by the abstract concepts considered in the last chapter but by a range of political, social and economic factors. Education is always inseparably connected with such wider trends in society, causally and consequentially, and to these we now turn.

Political attitudes to education

Political attitudes have been potent forces widening access to education. Chief among these at the beginning of the century was the gamut of attitudes associated with the National Efficiency movement.[1] The National Efficiency group was not in itself a political party but embraced adherents across the political spectrum from Imperialists like Lords Roberts and Milner, Conservatives like Joseph Chamberlain, Liberals like Haldane and Asquith through to Socialists like Sidney and Beatrice Webb. They and supposedly non-political civil servants like Robert Morant all found a common identity in their belief in the need for greater efficiency in the national life. This need was enhanced by the awareness of the relative decline of Britain's world supremacy since the 1880s in the face of Germany and the United States. Both countries presented a serious challenge to British industry, exports and technology, and Germany rivalled Britain in the scramble for colonial possessions in Africa and on the high seas. By the 1900s intense bad feeling between Britain and Germany was compounded by fear of 'Made in Germany' imports and suspicion of German military intentions.

Yet this was coupled with intense admiration for German science, technology and education, matching a similar healthy respect for American engineering, business 'know-how' and democratic education. This combination of the fear of challenging rivals and the admiration for their institutions, including education, shaped the attitudes of national efficiency advocates. They called for greater 'efficiency', which became a popular cliché word in the 1900s, whereby the British nation would preserve its standing against its rivals, often by imitating their best features, especially education.

National Efficiency attitudes found expression over wide areas of national life. They comprised a belief in the businessman and the expert, a devotion to the cult of science and a wish to correct its supposed neglect, a faith in the supremacy of the Anglo-Saxon race and its civilizing mission. Likewise it took many disparate forms characteristic of the 1900s – the adoption of American methods of scientific management, the building of battleships, the Boy Scout movement, attention to the physical health of the young by school meals and the medical inspection of school children. One of the staunchest planks in this broad platform was a passionate belief in education as a leading determinant of national resilience and strength.

At the school level the movement wanted to create access to secondary education for the talented lower classes through grammar schools and scholarships. Sidney Webb and Morant we have seen as especially involved in this. At a higher level, National Efficiency men were generally enthusiasts for scientific education in general and the civic universities in particular. This was especially so with Chamberlain, the prime mover in the creation of the University of Birmingham, the first chartered independent civic university, Haldane, the Chancellor of Bristol and creator of Imperial College and Webb, the reshaper of the University of London. Such a belief in education stemmed not so much from a conviction of the egalitarian rights of individuals. Indeed National Efficiency men were strong believers in competitive examinations, selective ladders and scholarships and the creaming off of élites. Rather their concern was for the needs of the state. The nation state of Britain could only face the industrial and military competition of its rivals by the most efficient garnering and deployment of its own intellectual talent. A well-ordered education system would train and select such talent from whatever social class it could. The most able would have the opportunity to serve the nation in scientific, industrial or military life which could no longer tolerate the socially eligible but intellectually incapable. Access to education based on competition and selection was thus vital not only for social justice for the individual but for the efficient competitiveness of the nation.

Indeed it was a common argument of the period that as in former times countries competed in trade based on their possession of raw materials, now their competitive effectiveness depended on the skill and intelligence which could be applied to these materials. It was the intelligence which gave the high value added content. This was most evidently so with the electrical, organic chemical and machine tool engineering products characteristic of the 1900s and into which Britain was trying to diversify out of the old basic industries. Trade competition was thus even more one between creative intellects which were the product of educational systems which in turn were shaped by government policies. National Efficiency advocates had accordingly no ideological objection to the role of the state in education. On the contrary it was a major force in achieving these educational, economic and other forms of efficiency which were their goal. These ideas were important in the 1900s and we have urgent need to return to them now.

Some Socialists like the Webbs were part of the National Efficiency circles but Socialists in general had their own motives for desiring greater access to education.[2] Firstly education was always seen as an agent of politicization. 'Educate, Agitate, Organize' was the slogan of the Social Democratic Federation, Britain's pioneer Marxist party, and is still to be seen on trade union banners to this day. The keeping of children in ignorance or in quietist subjection (as they might see it) to the ideologies of the Church and Victorian state which were designed to keep them in their place, was anathema to the Socialists. The more education working class children received beyond the elementary, the more they could acquire some social and political awareness of their class position. This might induce them to join trade unions, vote Labour or even become political activists. The Socialist Sunday Schools of the 1900s served this specific purpose. At a higher level various left-wing adult education movements of the 1900s like the Workers' Educational Association (1903), Ruskin College (1899) and its Marxist breakaway Central Labour College (1909) raised the awareness of the working classes through education. Conversely Eustace Percy, the Conservative President of the Board of Education in the 1920s was suspicious of the study of social history as inculcating in the working classes a consciousness of their own heritage. Percy was right. The more opportunities available to the working classes to gain access to education the more possible it was for the Left to create the politicized mass support which was to underpin Labour as a political force during the rest of the century.

Second, a strand in the Left also emphasized access to education as a vehicle of social mobility. This was evidently so with the Webbs and the Fabians' influence behind the 1902 Act. Going with this was the belief in the ladder of opportunity and scholarships and early notions of equality of opportunity of which we have seen something already. In this way increased educational opportunity would not so much politicize an inert working class as enable the selected cream of that class to climb up and out into some higher middle class and professional stratum. This emphasis within the Labour party showed itself not only over the 1902 Act and the scholarships provided by the London Technical Education Board, but in the attempts in the inter-war years to extend places for exelementary school children in grammar schools and in the implementation of the 1944 Act by the Labour government of 1945–51. Other sections of the Labour Party, further to the left, were less enthusiastic about the use of education as a catapult to eject an élite out of their class at the expense of leaving the mass behind in deprivation. Hence the SDF and School Board espousal of the higher elementary schools and their resentment of the 1902 Act and its aftermath with its sharp distinctions between grammar and elementary schools. Something of the same clash is seen in the 1960s between those wishing to continue developing the grammar school as the working class ladder to middle class success and those wishing to replace the whole system with the non-selective comprehensives providing catch-all opportunities.

Third, Socialists have seen that greater access to education has yielded all kinds of other material benefits. They have welcomed the successive raising of the school leaving age not only because it increased the amount of education received by their children but because it delayed their premature entry into industrial work. This had the ulterior effect of limiting the size of the labour force with beneficial implications for unemployment and wages. Furthermore various welfare benefits could be transmitted to children through schooling, notably school meals (1906), medical inspection (1907), even baths, boots and spectacles provided by some authorities, and school milk (1932). As the school came to be seen not only as an academic institution but as a centre of social welfare so was the motive greater for the Socialists wishing more children to attend it longer.

Fourth, a particular strain in Socialist attitudes was the belief in the value of education for its own sake, for self-fulfilment irrespective of the needs of job performance or the opportunities of social mobility. In Victorian times this was a rather upper middle class notion associated with the defence of liberal education in the universities. Here the arts subjects were justified not for the training they gave for specific occupations. Rather they were seen as fostering certain generalized intellectual and moral virtues associated with the formation of the gentleman. Conversely the education of the working classes was seen as serving more precise and manipulative purposes – conveying religious and patriotic values and the literacy, numerical and technical skills that would enable them to earn a living and serve the wider economy. This sharp distinction between what was regarded as suitable education for the leisured and for the working classes came to be resented by some of the latter. Among Socialists the belief in the intrinsic value of education had a long tradition through Robert Owen, the Co-operators, the Christian Socialists and William Morris. Late Victorian Socialists too claimed a right to education as the key to their cultural heritage and to the self-development and mind-nourishing which the gentleman classes had always claimed as a virtue of liberal education. These working class aspirations found expression in the adult education movements of the time, notably the WEA.

The First World War and the need to assert civilized values after the brutalities of war also widened the belief in the value of education for its own sake. The 1920 Committee on Scholarships noted that civilization suffered from a 'lack of broad and humanizing ideas that form the basis of enlightened citizenship' and that children needed a liberal secondary education to be open to 'the influence of high and generous ideals'.[3] It continued to fuel demands for secondary education for all. Here R. H. Tawney was an obvious direct link between Victorian liberal education ideals, transmitted through working class adult education, and the WEA and thence into demands for secondary education for all in the 1920s. This claim that education had a value in itself and that the working class had as much right to it on these grounds as the upper classes was an important shift. Now education was claimed by the working classes and not seen as something conceded or imposed from above for the benefits of social order and industrial efficiency.

The emphasis on education for its own sake was not without its counterproductive effects for the potential flow of talent. This was especially dangerous when the working classes accepted Victorian middle class notions of liberal education as appropriate to their needs when manifestly they were not. The 1908 Conference on Oxford and the Working Man suggested that working men needed education

> in order that they may face with wisdom the unsolved problems of their present position, not in order that they may escape to another . . . the task of the educationalists in the future must be not merely to make smoother the way of those who wish to rise to positions usually considered higher than that of the manual worker, but to ennoble the status of every class by supplying it, whatever its work and social conditions, with the form of culture appropriate to its needs.[4]

Here some rather comfortable middle class academics of left wing sympathies were placing before working men, considerably less comfortable than themselves, the ideal of education for culture as superior to that of education for self-advancement.

These ideas were not uncommon. The Liberal, H. A. L. Fisher, also believed that education should be valued as 'treasures of the mind' but 'not as a means of rising out of the working class' which was merely 'vulgar ambition'.[5] And George Tomlinson, a Socialist and another President of the Board of Education like Fisher, held that 'Education isn't a means of getting a better job than Dad'.[6] There are uneasy moral issues here. It is open to question whether many working men might not have been using access to education as a self-indulgence whereas their duty to themselves and their families might have been better served by clambering up the ladders of opportunity. There is in Socialism a certain streak of naivety in its attitude to education. This stems from the French *philosophes* of the eighteenth century, Helvétius and Condorcet and their exaggerated (*l'éducation peut tout*) beliefs in the power of education to transform men and bring about progress and perfectibility. These ideas were transmitted into British Socialism directly through Robert Owen who was profoundly influenced by Helvétius in particular. It has left the Socialist tradition and some working men with an equally exaggerated view of the importance of education – almost any kind of education – for their own position. The danger of this has been an excessive reverence for education for its own sake rather than as a springboard access to upward mobility.

The Conservatives too have a tradition of widening the access to education. Indeed several of the major legislative advances are the product of their administrations. Balfour's 1902 Act, the 1936 Act and the Butler Act of 1944 were direct Conservative achievements. The Fisher Act of 1918 was the product of the Liberal and Conservative Coalition of December 1916. The successive raising of the school-leaving age throughout the century has owed much to the Conservatives – to 14 (1918), to 15 (1936 and 1944), to 16 by Margaret Thatcher in 1972. The Party has also had several politicians who have also been practising academics and who have devoted part of their political careers to education – Eustace Percy (later Vice-Chancellor of Newcastle), Edward Boyle (later Vice-Chancellor of Leeds), Quintin Hogg and Keith Joseph (Fellows of All Souls), R. A. Butler (Fellow of Corpus Christi College Cambridge) and the respected historian and headmaster Dr Rhodes Boyson have all led or served in the Board of Education, Ministry of Education or Department of Education and Science. It is also part of Conservative philosophy to care passionately about certain educational issues. There is a genuine concern for quality expressed through the defence of the grammar schools and the best public schools. Conservatives have defended liberty and the freedom of choice embodied in the rights of parents to send children to independent schools or to choose a neighbourhood state school. They also believe in the need for a strong moral, religious and patriotic content in education and in the necessity of linking education with industry and promoting technical studies. All these preoccupations have been beneficial drives in the development of education and access to it.

Yet there are certain factors in the Conservative position which have worked against the developments that we are concerned with. First, the Conservatives used to be regarded as the non-intellectual or even the 'stupid' party[7] with a concomitant scepticism about the value of education. This has become less true as men with higher levels of professional training have replaced farmers, gentlemen of leisure and family firm businessmen as the chief element among Tory MPs. Indeed in the last twenty years there has been a spate of intellectualizing about Conservative philosophy with appeals to Burke and Disraeli and so forth. Yet to a much lesser extent than Socialism (with Marx) and Liberalism (with Bentham, Mill, T.H. Green) is Conservatism a creed of the Book.

Secondly, Conservatives, unlike Socialists, tend to be sceptical about teachers and their 'professional' pretensions which they see as linked uneasily with left-wing trade unionism. The often working class and lower middle class origins of state school teachers diminishes their credibility in the eyes of the party of the ruling classes. Timothy Raison expresses frankly the suspicion that 'many teachers are people who have opted out of the rat race'.[8] Their lack of the high intellectual attainments of the true professions or of the entrepreneurial qualities of the businessmen diminishes the regard in which they are held. This feeling among teachers of being contemptuously undervalued underlies much of the troubles in education in the last few years.

Third, Conservatives are also basically sceptical about the role of education as a mechanism of achieving equality. For Socialists this was fundamental, especially after Crosland's book of 1956 which pointed to educational reform, rather than nationalization or other policies, as the key to equality. For Socialists widening access was a major element in social engineering. Conservatives do not believe in equality as a goal (for reasons we have seen in the previous chapter) and in any case, as the former Secretary of State for Education Sir Keith Joseph has observed, 'for the Conservatives education is not about equality'.[9] Indeed Sir Keith published a book specifically attacking equality in the year the Conservative government took office in 1979.

Finally and most important, education, far from being a leading edge in Conservative strategy, must take a lower priority than other considerations – defence, the search for growth in the economy through the limitation of inflation, the curbing of the spheres of influence and expenditure of the state.[10] In particular, where the demands of educational expenditure clash with the need to restrain public expenditure to maintain low prices, interest rates and taxation then education must take a subordinate role. Indeed cuts in education have often been used as a deflator in the economy in this century – in 1921, with the Geddes cuts in 1922, the teachers' salary cuts of 1932, the cuts in teachers' real income in the early 1950s and mid 1980s. Behind all this has been in recent years the broader ideological commitment to the diminished role of the state. For Sir Keith Joseph as both the leader of the educational service and the leading advocate of the diminished participation of the state and of restrained public expenditure, the tensions between the two roles have been particularly acute. At a time when excessive private sector wage settlements and bank lending to consumers are out of control and undermine the anti-inflationary strategies of the government, education has been accorded a lower priority and even a depressive role in the overall situation.

In recent years the Conservatives have lacked a certain credibility as guardians of state education and there is an alienation between teachers at all levels and the Party, which worries some Conservatives.[11] However this is not inevitable nor necessarily long lasting. Yet if the Left has had a high idealistic view of the importance of education verging on the naive, the view of the Right has more often been sceptical and ambivalent.

The stimulus of war

In this century the experience of war has also profoundly affected access to education. In general terms it has done so in four main ways. The struggle and suffering of war raises expectations among the people of the winning side that some reward should result from victory. All classes tend to hold common aspirations for a joint share in a better world. Indeed such a prospect encourages the lower orders to tolerate the war weariness and sacrifice which is usually their lot. Second, war tends to bring different social classes into close proximity: officers and men in battle; comfortable and deprived in home-front evacuation schemes. In the past this had the effect of heightening the sense of deprivation of the poorer classes and, more important, often awakened a sense of compassion and social conscience among the richer. This made them more willing to support social reform in the post-war years that they would not have hitherto contemplated. Third, wartime industrial activity and women working often raised the incomes and living standards of the working classes. The raised expectations spilled over into greater demands for education for their children which they were now often able to pay for themselves. This was evidently so in the First World War. Finally, the actual conduct of the war itself required higher educational levels on the part of the common soldier. In the Second World War much care was taken to educate the troops in an understanding of the issues for which they were fighting. In both wars the vast amount of technical training of troops in a range of matters such as map-reading and gun-laying both placed a greater importance on education and was a process of education in itself. In all these ways the two world wars aroused a greater awareness of the importance of education and led to a widening of its availability.

In the 1914–18 War the immediate effect of hostilities was adverse as some 20,000 elementary schoolteachers were called up and not entirely replaced with 17,500 women. Children too were drawn into the war, being used in agriculture and other industry as early as 11 to the damage of their education. Yet more widely the war focused attention on education and heightened public awareness of its importance. The demands of war for science and technology in a whole range of products from aircraft and shells to optical lenses and dyes were met by university and industrial scientists. This resulted in a greater appreciation of science and of the education that lay behind it. This greatly raised the public appreciation of the civic universities. Never again would Oxford be as negligent of science as it had been before 1914. Meanwhile the numbers of undergraduates of all universities rose sharply in the inter-war years over those of the Edwardian generation. However casual British industry had been about the education and skill of its labour force in the years before the war, the war brought a lethal urgency to the problem. Truck drivers, map-readers, navigators, required by the thousand from ex-elementary school boys showed the need for competent arithmetical as well as literacy skills. They were to be matched against the products of the most renowned schoolmasters of Europe, those of the German Volksschulen.

Public pressure for improved education crystallized. The *Times Education Supplement* in 1915 started calling for a universal system of secondary education. Haldane continued to stress the importance of continuation classes and teacher training which the Lewis Report of 1917 reiterated. The Labour Party too became very concerned about education during the war. The TUC demanded equality of educational opportunity and in 1916 a conference of trade unionists met at Bradford to draw up the Bradford Charter. This called for free and compulsory education to 16 and its programme was adopted as Labour Party policy in January 1917. Geoffrey Sherington calls this 'Labour's new awakening to the importance of education'.[12] By the end of 1916 concern for education benefited from the wider concern for post-war reform in health and housing. The Reconstruction Committee had an education panel and this called for a raising of the school-leaving age to 15 and ultimately to 16 followed by part-time continuation education to 18. Intermixed with all these pressures was the wartime belief that those who had borne the brunt of the war both as soldiers and on the home front deserved condign reward for their sacrifice. 'Homes for Heroes', female suffrage and educational reform would be expressions of material gratitude no less than the Cenotaph and the War Memorial halls and parks throughout the land.

The 1914–18 War increased the access of the working classes to secondary education. Pupils in grammar schools rose from 187,000 in 1914 to 337,000 by 1920.[13] Full employment and higher earnings, with ample opportunities for women to work, had swollen working class family budgets and raised their real wages for the first time since the 1890s. Letting the child go to secondary school was one of the ways in which this improved standard of living was enjoyed. The war also brought an enhanced awareness of the importance of literacy itself. The avid desire for war information stimulated the reading of newspapers and the writing of letters between those at home and relatives at the front. 'Communications from husbands and sons, official forms and later ration books all made hitherto unknown demands upon the unlettered or near literate'. Accordingly the bottle of Stephens ink, writing paper and pen became as much part of the stock of the corner shop as the newspaper and John Bull periodical.[14] The authority structures of the army – officers, NCOs and other ranks – also brought home to people in a highly formalized way the realities underlying peace-time social structure. A grammar school boy might become an officer; an elementary schoolboy never.

All this culminated in the H.A.L. Fisher Education Act of 1918 which embodied many of the demands floated during the war. This raised the school-leaving age to 14 and provided for continuation schools to be attended part time by teenagers who had started work. There was nothing as radical in this as the 1902 Act or the Hadow reorganization and some of the measures were swept away by the economy measures of the early 1920s. But the raised expectations of the war heightened an appreciation of the value of education which was to be continued in the claims for secondary education for all in the 1920s.

If the long-term educational effects of the First World War were limited by the subsequent recessions the impact of the Second World War was more decisive.[15] Various factors began to shift public opinion towards sympathy with working class welfare and education. The Blitz of 1940–1 increased a concern for the plight of the poor and dispossessed which was met with welfare centres and hostels. There was a great increase in the provision of school meals and nursery schools for evacuees in 1940. Both before and after the Blitz the evacuation of school children from city slums to rural areas where they could be billeted in the larger houses of the relatively comfortable had an effect. It brought home to many who had enjoyed a comfortable 1930s just how deprived many of the children of England were. Their lousy heads, malnourished frames, toilet habits, foul language and illiterate ignorance were a shock. The sharp rise in juvenile delinquency after 1939 added to the concern about children.

Several bodies and organizations began to take an interest in welfare planning and education. In 1941 R.A. Butler founded the Conservative Post War Problems Committee. Its educational sub-committee reported in 1942 and emphasized the importance of national education in developing a strong sense of patriotism. It would create such qualities as 'the will to work, pride in occupation regardless of social or monetary reward, the self-discipline acquired through submission to discipline and the desire to find salvation from selfishness in service'.[16] If the Conservatives were interested in education for patriotism the Churches were shifting to the Left. Anglican bishops and clergy met for a conference at Malvern College in January 1941 that revealed a strong Socialist bent. William Temple was a Labour supporter and moved from York to Canterbury in January 1942 to be succeeded by Cyril Garbett who shared his political views. Temple's *Christianity and Social Order* (1942) with its advocacy of a higher school-leaving age arose directly from this ecclesiastical climate of opinion.

Another group emerging from the war was the All Souls Group convened in June 1941 by Dr W.G.S. Adams, Warden of All Souls, to discuss post-war education. Its distinguished members were all to be leading figures in English education in the post-war years. At the time 'its deliberations were of seminal importance in helping to shape the pattern of wartime educational legislation and post-war educational developments'.[17] R.A. Butler was a guest visitor at their discussions and he made available to them the confidential Green Memorandum 1941 in preparation for the 1943 White Paper which preceded the 1944 Act.

In 1942 there was a marked centralizing of political views on to a middle ground of consensus. There was much talk of the 'retreat from Party', and a softening of party lines. A body seeking to capitalize on this middle ground was the Common Wealth Party founded in July 1942 as a merger of earlier groups by J.B. Priestley and Sir Richard Acland. Their stance was a kind of middle class liberal socialism. 'The People's War' was a phrase of theirs expressing the notion that it was the common people of England who were bearing the brunt of the conflict and that their social needs deserved attention during the war and in the subsequent peace. Highly idealistic about post-war reconstruction they believed that the 'People's War' should be followed by planning for a 'People's Peace'. As J.B. Priestley put it, the new world should be one 'where everyone has a reasonable chance and nobody has any special privileges'.[18]

The Common Wealth Party especially placed much hope in the

Beveridge Report of 1942. Although this was concerned with Social Insurance Beveridge did refer to education. He identified the five dragons which had blighted the lives of the poor in the 1930s and which would have to be slain in the post-war years – Want, Disease, Idleness, Squalor and Ignorance. The dragon of Ignorance, 'which no democracy can afford among its citizens' as Beveridge put it, would have to be tackled by a new Education Act.[19] By the end of the war the propagation of the Beveridge Report and its ideals owed less to the waning Common Wealth Party than to the thriving ABCA. The ABCA (Army Bureau of Current Affairs) founded in 1941 was the Army's adult education unit and was itself a product of the war. Its purpose was to produce pamphlets on issues of the day for use in discussion groups. This gave the troops a clearer democratic view of war aims and international affairs. The pamphlet on the Beveridge Report attracted enormous interest, to such an extent that Churchill feared that it was raising exaggerated expectations for social reform after the war. His withdrawal of the pamphlet is thought to have indicated to the troops that they could not look to the Tories to carry out such a programme of social reconstruction in peacetime and this in turn contributed to the Labour landslide victory of 1945.

In all these ways, from pragmatic educational responses to the Blitz and evacuation through to major shifts in ideology, the Second World War marked a sharper break with the 1930s in education than the First World War had with the 1900s. Moreover, whereas many of the hopes of the 1918 Act were blighted by the recessions of the inter-war years, those of 1944 were to be followed by a generation of development and fruition.

The role of the state

Apart from the intense episodes of war, the long term acceptance of the positive role of the state in education has also widened educational opportunities throughout the century. This has been increasingly so since the 1830s when government grants for elementary education began in 1833 and a tough Factory Act in the same year enforced compulsory education for factory children. In those days even the dominant ideology of Benthamite Utilitarian-ism, generally hostile to state intervention, made a significant exception in the case of education. Indeed it was staunch pressure of the Benthamite group in parliament which had helped to bring about the state grants in the first place. The Tories too then believed in the state's duty towards public education and it was Tory Anglicans who brought about the measures for the com-pulsory education of factory and mining children. In the late nineteenth century, from the 1880s *laissez faire,* liberalism was moved in the direction of collectivism by the writings of T.H. Green, Oxford don and city councillor. He popularized the view that freedom was not a negative attribute and not merely the absence of state control or interference with free will and motiva-tion. On the contrary the lives of many poor people were imprisoned by their poverty and ignorance from which they had insufficient personal power to escape. Freedom for them could only be achieved by the state striking off the shackles which bound them. The eradication of ignorance by the positive intervention of the state was as much a prerequisite of true liberty as the eradication of poverty. T.H. Green had a direct influence on H.A.L. Fisher, the architect of the 1918 Education Act.

In practice by the turn of the century the principle of the state's duty towards education was well established. There was com-pulsory (1880) and free (1891) elementary state education, state inspection (1840), state grants for universities (1889) and for students to attend them and state secondary schools from 1902. By 1920 it was possible for a government report to claim that:

> the state has a responsibility for the provision to its citizens of the means of education is a principle which it is needless for us to discuss . . . it has been accepted and acted upon to an extent that places it now outside the sphere of controversy.[20]

Accordingly the acceptance of the right and duty of the state to provide education and even to compel it for the nation's children has led not only to successive raising of the compulsory school-leaving age but also to increasing levels of government finance for education out of generally rising levels of national wealth. We can see this from various estimates:[21]

Table 41: Central and local government expenditure on education

	UK central government expenditure on education		Total local government expenditure on education		Total central and local government spending on education
	as % of total central government expenditure	as % of National Income	as % of total local government expenditure	as % of National Income	as % of National Income
1900	8.49	0.69	11.4	0.76	1.45
1905	10.43	0.88	14.43	1.55	2.43
1910	11.41	0.90	18.62	1.74	2.64
1915	3.61	0.78	20.28	1.55	2.33
1920	2.59	1.08	20.18	1.18	2.26
1925	6.49	1.22	17.90	2.18	3.40
1930	6.41	1.27	17.19	2.61	3.88
1935	6.73	1.28	17.21	2.54	3.82
1940	4.50	1.06	16.29	2.14	3.20
1945	1.39	1.02	17.36	1.76	2.78
1950	6.85	1.34	24.18	2.97	4.31
1955	7.48	2.18	26.61	2.57	4.75
1959	9.63	2.67	32.20	3.74	6.41

Table 42: Public expenditure on education as a percentage of National Income

Hicks[22]		Vaizey[23]	
1900	1.1	1920	1.2
1910	1.1	1925	2.1
1923	2.2	1930	2.3
1933	2.7	1935	2.4
1936	2.5	1940	2.0
1949	2.5	1945	1.7
1951	3.0	1948	2.5
		1950	2.7
		1955	2.8
		1965	3.9

Table 43: Public expenditure on education as a percentage of Gross National Product

Patten[24]		Pollard[25]	
1950	2.8	1930s	2.5
1980	6.1	1950s	3.0
		mid-1960s	5.0
		1980	6.0

The trend of the various estimates is clear and within narrow limits fairly consistent. Public expenditure on state education has remained a steady 21–24 per cent of government spending on social services,[26] but has risen as a proportion of all government expenditure. It has also risen as a percentage of the National Income from around one per cent in 1900s to three to four per cent by the mid-century to about six per cent by the 1980s. This steady growth has been an underlying factor in the widening access to education.

The demand for education

So far in this chapter we have been concerned with some factors influencing the expanding supply of education – political attitudes, the influence of war and the increase of public finance for education. Yet increased access to education is also influenced by a rising demand for this service and this in turn has been subject to some subtly changing factors during the century.

Increasing personal wealth, for example, has fuelled the demand for education. It has allowed a range of consumption from grammar school education before 1944, to public school and university eduction throughout the period, especially among the middle classes. Total UK consumers' expenditure at constant prices has risen by nearly two and a half times from £9,079m. in 1900 to £22,278m. by 1968. Since this has outstripped population growth, consumers' expenditure per head has risen markedly.[27]

Table 44: *Consumers' expenditure in Britain, 1901, 1966*

	Consumers' expenditure £m. at constant 1958 and 1963 prices	Population	Consumers' expenditure per head
1901	9,191	36,999,946	£248.40
1966	21,249	52,303,810	£406.26

Consumers' expenditure measures all types of personal consumption. 'Constant prices' takes account of inflation and measures the real increase of expenditure.

The flourishing state of the public schools and the great increase in the numbers going to university have been sustained by these trends.

Furthermore, using part of one's consumption for the education of children is perceived as worth while given the changing occupational structure of the labour force in the century. From before the First World War to the 1980s it has been the educated white collar, managerial, clerical and professional classes whose proportions in the overall occupational structure have increased, while the manual workers have relatively diminished:[28]

Table 45: The occupational structure in Britain, 1911–79 (percentages)

	1911	1921	1931	1951	1961	1971	1979
Professional	4.05	4.53	4.60	6.63	9.0	11.07	17.1
Employers and managers	10.14	10.46	10.36	10.50	10.10	12.43	12.9
Clerical	4.84	6.72	6.97	10.68	12.70	13.90	16.0
Foremen and manual workers	80.97	78.29	78.07	72.19	68.10	62.60	54.0

This occupational shift is characteristic of advanced countries becoming richer but it has proceeded even further in Britain than in the more affluent Germany, France and Japan. Educated professionals have vastly increased in absolute numbers. Between 1911 and 1971 major (A1) professions like engineers multiplied by a factor of 17, scientists by 15.4, accountants by 7 and doctors by 2.2. Between 1921 and 1971 minor (A2) professions like male social workers multiplied by 22, female social workers by 20, male nurses by 17, and male teachers by 4 times.[29] By contrast the Edwardian reservoirs of agricultural labourers, domestic servants and porters diminished over the century while manual workers increased scarcely at all. Guy Routh surmises that the bright young men who became Edwardian shop assistants were the sort of people who with more education sixty years later became teachers, nurses and draughtsmen.[30] The men behind the counter vanished, along with the ploughmen and the porters and the upstairs maids.

It was consistently evident that expanding job opportunities did not lie in the manual occupations requiring only an elementary education. The brute strength of the 'ox man' and the mindless conscientiousness of the 'ant woman', in Sir Michael Clapham's vivid phrase, were being phased out of the labour force.[31] The dynamic growth areas were the higher professionals and managers from the public schools, grammar schools and universities, the clerks from the grammar schools and the technicians from the junior and senior technical schools. The awareness of this increasing disparity of opportunities was a further spur to parents wanting good secondary and higher education for their children as gateways to expanding careers.

The rise of the managerial class is in turn reflected in the rise of salaries as a proportion of national income. Whereas wages remained roughly constant around 40 per cent of the national income between 1900 and 1968 yet the proportion of salaries (as opposed to wages, profits, rent, etc.) has risen from 9.1 per cent to 35.4 per cent in the same period.[32]

Yet the shift from lower to higher occupations has also been accompanied by a narrowing of pay differentials within the spectrum across the century:[33]

Table 46: Salaries in 1978 as a multiple of those in 1913–14

	Men		Women	
Professional higher	× 26	⎫	–	⎫
lower	× 35	⎬ × 33.6	× 44	⎬ × 53.5
Managers	× 40	⎭	× 63	⎭
Manual skilled	× 41	⎫	× 51	⎫
semi-skilled	× 55	⎬ × 50	× 47	⎬ × 59.6
unskilled	× 54	⎭	× 81	⎭

The incentive to gain access to education as a means of moving into the expanding professional and managerial jobs was partly the higher incomes of the latter. But that incentive was moderated rather than intensified by the narrowing differentials.

This narrowing was itself a product of increasing access to education as well as of a changing public attitude in favour of greater equality. Recruitment to the higher professions before the twentieth century was largely limited to those who could afford the private costs of public school and Oxford and Cambridge. The widening access to grammar schools and universities through public grants has increased the supply of potential professionals and kept their rise in incomes modest. Lower professions like teaching have been flooded with entrants and suffered a substantial reduction in their salaries relative to other groups. The exodus from less skilled jobs, as young people have used education to move upwards, has led to a marked relative increase in their incomes. This in turn has made what used formerly to be regarded as modest jobs very attractive to people with higher education. Graduates now rightly think of the police, fire service or working as a chef as desirable, demanding and rewarding future careers.

However as real inequality between the social classes has diminished over the twentieth century so, it is argued, the perception of relative deprivation has increased.[34] Feelings of envy or the desire to emulate are only felt between social groups near enough to make such feelings realistic. Nobody is envious of the Queen. Similarly very few Edwardian labourers or agricultural workers expected their children to get to a grammar school, even fewer to university and none at all to public school. Yet the minimal expectation was matched by a minimal grievance that such benefits were beyond them. As some of the lower classes were gradually drawn into secondary and higher education by the Morant arrangements, Hadow, 1944 and so forth, so the aspirations of their peers rose. This undermined the normal working class assumptions that secondary and higher education were not part of their goals, failure to achieve which was thus not a matter for regret or reproach.

By the 1940s and 1950s equalization had proceeded to the extent that most working class parents desired a grammar school place for their children. Raised aspirations reached also to higher education. Gary Runciman found in 1962 that 82 per cent of manual workers wanted a university education for their children, ranging narrowly from 79 per cent of the poorest to 89 per cent of the most affluent manual workers. This proportion was, moreover, very similar to that of the non-manual workers, 88 per cent of whom wanted their children to go to university.[35] Greater real equality had led to an equalizing of aspirations. Yet nothing like 82 per cent of the working class would achieve university entrance: 70 per cent would have their expectations frustrated. The very fact that aspirations (which would scarcely have existed in the 1900s), had been raised but would largely not be met, in itself provided a pressure of demand. Its frustration provided on-going pressure for change.

This entailed a shifting of working class priorities away from a preference for traditional manual jobs towards occupations requiring a higher level of education. For example, when offered a choice of post for their son, either a foreman's at £20 a week or a schoolteacher's at £15, all middle class respondents chose the latter. Older (over 45) working class men preferred the better paid foreman's job but the younger generation of working class, aged 21–45, would have chosen to be a less well paid teacher.[36] It suggested that the younger generation of the working class were moving their priorities away from traditional working class values more in the direction of those of the middle classes. This entailed a preference for education-based occupations even at a financial cost. It also suggested a greater appreciation of and desire for education among the class traditionally deprived of it and indifferent to it.

Education and social mobility

As all these points suggest, there has been an intimate interconnection between access to education and social mobility in Britain in the twentieth century. Britain is a fairly fluid society: a little more than half of adults stay in the same social class in which they were born yet 'a very substantial minority of Englishmen and Welshmen in the last generation have been socially mobile (44.6 per cent)'.[37] It is actually the working class which is most self-perpetuating and the middle class most open to the *arriviste* within the expanded professional and technical occupations.

Yet the possibility of being an *arriviste* – or yuppy (young upwardly mobile professional) in the inelegant term of the 1980s – depended a good deal on education. We can look at the educational experience of the stable middle class and of those moving upwards into the middle class as A. H. Halsey shows:[38]

Table 47: The educational experience of the middle class and the upwardly mobile, 1972 (percentages)

	Private primary schooling	Selective secondary schooling	School exams	Some FE qualifi- cation	University degree
Stable middle class	32	88.4	82.0	33.1	29.8
Lower middle to middle	11.7	67.9	62.1	34.1	13.5
Working to middle	1.6	63.1	58.5	32.3	12.8

This may be contrasted with that of the downwardly mobile to the working class and with the stable working class itself:

Table 48: The educational experience of the working class and the downwardly mobile, 1972 (percentages)

Middle to working	3.8	33.5	15.1	7.0	0.5
Lower middle to working	3.0	21.9	8.1	1.8	0.1
Stable working class	0.6	14.7	4.6	0.4	0.1

At all points of comparison the downwardly mobile and the lower classes were vastly lower in educational experience and achievement than the upwardly mobile and middle classes. Education is obviously far from the only determinant of mobility but it is not to undervalue qualities of individual character, personality and luck to recognize that it is statistically a very potent one. Cause and effect work in both directions here. As those with the best education rise upwards to higher social classes so they in turn appreciate its benefits sufficiently to ensure (buy?) the best education for their offspring. The widening opportunities in the professional-managerial reaches of the occupational structure accessible only to the better educated act as the incentive. The penalty is not only a *déclassé* descent to the working class but a precipitate fall beyond it to the poverty of unemployment.

In this chapter we have looked away from education directly to consider some of the political, economic and sociological factors influencing the context of access to education. Now we want to look more widely in another direction to see by some international comparisons how typical have been England's problems or laggard its performance.

VI

A Sideways Look: Foreign Comparisons

Britain's experience in extending access to education through the century is not of course unique. Many of the features of this expansion were shared with other European, Western or industrialized countries. It is accordingly worth while placing Britain in this comparative context to highlight not only similarities but those areas where we have been laggard in performance and have something to learn from friends and competitors.

Secondary education

Since all countries with which it is meaningful to compare Britain have had compulsory primary education in this century there is nothing remarkable here, but comparative differences do emerge at the secondary level. Proportions of secondary pupils per total population have grown steadily in Europe during the century.[1]

Table 49: *Percentage of secondary school pupils per population in Europe, 1900–70*

	1900	1910	1920	1930	1950	1960	1970
Belgium	0.46	0.48	0.69	0.60	1.52	2.62	3.39
France	0.26	0.32	–	0.80	1.84	3.21	5.58
Germany	–	1.56	1.71	1.54	1.30	1.78	2.96
Italy	0.28	0.47	1.05	0.75	2.33	2.79	4.00
Sweden	0.36	0.43	0.58	0.68	1.43	3.5	5.13
Netherlands	0.25	0.35	0.47	1.34	2.19	3.76	4.50
UK	–	0.44	1.15	1.26	4.02	6.08	6.38

Taking another criterion we can see the growth of secondary schooling in the major European countries in the following table.[2]

Educational Opportunity and Social Change in England

Table 50: Percentage of secondary school pupils per age group in Europe, 1898–1968

	France Enrolment in 6th grade as a % of total 11–17 age group	Baccalaureat per age group		Germany Secondary pupils as a % of total 11–19 age group		Abitur per age group		England and Wales Persons aged 15–18 at school as a % of that total age group	
1898	2.5	1900	0.9	c. 1900	2.7	1900	1.2	1900	0.3
		1910	1.2			1910	1.1		
1911	2.6	1920	1.3	1911	3.2	1920	1.4	1911	1.5
1921	3.5	1930	3.3	1921	6.0	1930	2.3	1921	3.2
1931	6.9	1940	4.5	1931	8.8			1931	6.0
1936	7.2							1938	6.6
1946	14.6								
1951	17.3	1950	5.4	1950	9.1	1950	5.7	1951	12.5
1956	24.6			1060	12.4	1960	11.2	1961	19.6
1961	42.3							1968	30.0

The figures are not of course comparable across the columns but they severally illustrate the surging growth of entry into secondary education in the leading European countries of the time. However, the problem in Britain by the end of the 1960s was in keeping pupils in school beyond the school-leaving age. There had been a marked increase in staying on into the sixth form in England in the 1950s and 1960s, but none the less England was somewhat behind in this respect.[4]

Table 51: Comparison of percentages of an age group enrolled as full-time students, 1969

	16-year-olds	17-year-olds
USA	86.3	75.6
France	50.0	36.7
Sweden	26.6	15.2
Italy	25.5	19.0
Germany	26.5	16.9
England and Wales	25.7	13.7

Whereas the proportions of 16-year-olds at school were very similar throughout Europe, when it came to 17-year-olds England was perceptibly a back runner. In consequence the proportions of an age group fully qualified for admission to university reflected this.[4]

Table 52: Comparative percentages of an age group qualified for admission to university, 1965

USA	76.7
Japan	50.7
Norway	18.6
Sweden	13.6
France	13.2
England and Wales	9.2
Germany	6.7

As regards primary and secondary education across the compulsory age ranges the UK was in line with the rest of NW Europe. Most NW European countries provided 10–11,000 hours of compulsory education in a schooling career whereas the UK provided 11,716. E. F. Denison in his influential growth study (1967) found the UK's position quite satisfactory, experiencing a good increase in the quality of education of the labour force which – he considered – would provide a favourable climate for future economic growth.[5]. It is ironic in the light of subsequent develop-ments that the country over which he was most pessimistic in this regard was Germany.

Teenage vocational education

That Germany has markedly outstripped Britain in spite of rather similar levels of primary and secondary education is largely due to another factor. The major fault in the British system is in the treatment of non-academic post-school teenagers. This is where we had most to learn from the Germans and our failure to do so since the First World War has resulted in one of the gravest weaknesses of our present position.

From the nineteenth century the Germans had developed Trade Continuation Schools which received children from the elementary Volksschulen at 12 or 14 and kept them until the age of 18. This compulsorily reinforced and developed their education part time in the years when they were starting paid work between elementary school and military service. It ensured that children destined for the world of work rather than for secondary education did not fall out of the educational system altogether. Their literacy and mathematics were sustained and extended. Further education was available in military service and Fachschulen for those aspiring to be foremen or small entrepreneurs. The ablest, finding a late-burgeoning technological and academic ability, might then go to the Technical High Schools. This tradition of providing a conveyor belt of on-going education as part of a career in industry from the age of 14 was one of the great strengths of the German education system, the formation of its labour force and German industrial competitiveness. Attention in England tended to emphasize the achievements of German chemists and their prestigious university chemistry departments and industrial research laboratories. No less important was this vastly less glamorous area nurturing the academically mediocre, workaday, working class teenager returning to the classroom grimy from his labours. Britain has never taken this problem sufficiently seriously, let alone found a solution for it.

Sir Michael Sadler publicized the German system of continuation schools in 1908 and provision of such schools was included in the Fisher Act in 1918. Yet, as we have seen, these vanished in the education cuts of the early 1920s. The Junior Technical Schools had likewise emerged in the 1900s but they were insufficiently encouraged by the Hadow Report and the reorganization of the 1920s and 1930s and far too much underplayed in the implementation of the Butler Act of 1944. The failure to develop Junior Technical Schools and Trade Continuation Schools has left Britain with a whole network missing from what should be a modern educational system. It has been the chief difference between ourselves and the Germans and one of our chief weaknesses *vis-à-vis* them.

This is belatedly coming to be appreciated. In Britain 82 per cent of children leave school at 16 and 68 per cent of those leave full-time education altogether. Forty per cent leave with no qualifications at all. By contrast, in Japan only four per cent leave before 18, in Germany just under ten per cent and in the USA just over ten per cent.[6] The English Junior Technical School barely got going and was then swallowed up in the comprehensives in the 1960s. The Germans by contrast continued to believe in the three-tier system and selection which they had developed in the nineteenth century. The Gymnasium or grammar school takes a fifth of children for academic education while the Realschule takes another quarter for a more practical and technical education. More distinctively the Hauptschule takes the less academically able children (about a half of an age group) from the age of 10 to 15 to prepare them for trades. These Hauptschule pupils also spend part of their week in an Ausbildungszentrum or apprentice centre working alongside the kind of apprentices they in turn expect to become when they leave. The majority of Hauptschule pupils go on to some further education and take certificates from their school covering a range of mathematics, sciences, German, history and geography. The certificate in turn is the passport to apprenticeship.[7] Beyond the Hauptschule is the Berufsschule or vocational training school for apprentices actually in work. Blake Baker describes the one in Cologne for 800 day release young people:[8]

Serious girls and youths sit behind complicated machines learning to grind spectacle lenses. Others tile bathrooms and weld plastic lagging. Bricklayers learn carpentry and carpenters learn bricklaying. Twenty miles away in Bonn at Fleischhauer, a large Volkswagen maintenance depot, a young second year apprentice dismantles and re-assembles an engine for real, not for practice. He, too, goes to a Berufsschule for one or two days a week to learn servicing of other makes.

Always present in schools or firms is a Meister, a master craftsman to supervise work, answer questions, help solve problems, maintain strict discipline . . .

In 1984 German firms provided over 700,000 apprenticeships and 97 per cent of school leavers, who were not proceeding further, were placed in one. Sixty per cent of the German labour force has attained apprenticeship or similar intermediate qualification compared with 30 per cent at most in Britain. Moreover, German vocational training is much better in mathematics-using areas, English youth in the lower half of the ability range being some two years behind its German counterpart in mathematical skills.[9] Accordingly German youth unemployment is the lowest in the EEC. The Germans have been much better at educating the lowest half of the ability range and they have successfully developed from within that half much of the technically skilled labour force on which their industrial strength rests.

The same is true in Switzerland.[10] There, the Gymnasium takes the top 10 per cent of academic ability but the rest are not consigned as 'failures'. The Secondarschule prepares students for white-collar jobs in banks and offices, the Realschule for practical trades in draughtsmanship and so forth, while at a lower level the Oberschule prepares pupils for such jobs as building work. Britain has much to learn from the Germanic nations on how to deal with non-academic teenagers. The academically able 10 or 20 per cent is creamed off, as used to be the case in England, but the rest are given technical and vocational education orientated to their future careers and to the needs of the nation. Moreover, they keep on with this longer and often in ways integrated with the world of work. Britain too will have to move more in this direction if there is to be hope of industrial regeneration and the reduction of hopeless teenage and early adult unemployment.

The Japanese system too seems better at catering for both the academic and the practical in divergent streams. The 6-3-3-4 system begins with six years in an elementary school, three years each in a junior and senior high school followed, for the ablest, by four years at university. The sharp division comes at 15 when children proceed either to a senior high school en route for university or to a vocational school. Very few actually leave at 15, only about six per cent, the vast majority proceeding either on to the academic or vocational route. The academic route entails the 'examination hell' of entry to senior high school, university and graduation, a path taken by about a third of Japanese youth. But almost all the rest continue to be developed in vocational schools.

A recent visitor describes this kind of education.[11]

> Those children who do not aspire to university sometimes opt to go to a vocational establishment. We visited the Seto Ceramic Upper Secondary School and the atmosphere here was very pleasant and much more relaxed. They still had resolute determination and group dominance, but it was a chosen course. The work appeared to be of a high standard and we saw industrial skills being trained (e.g. engineering, draughtsmanship) as well as pottery. In another building girls were learning secretarial duties – the typewriters are incredible with about 200 symbols, also some computer work. Later we visited Okazaki Stonemason Complex Co-operative Association which runs a course at their works for apprentices from a similar school. Once these pupils are qualified they can be employed by the Co-operative as well as running a small shop of their own to sell their work.

Mathematics (in which the Japanese are world leaders) and science studies are maintained and, also in contrast to England, teachers are highly paid and respected professional people.

Various surveys and criteria for recent years show Britain's backwardness in this regard. In the following surveys by individual scholars or official organizations various geographical areas are referred to. Britain or Great Britain consists of England, Scotland and Wales. The United Kingdom is Great Britain and Northern Ireland. Sometimes England and Wales or merely England alone is the unit. For the mid-1970s the percentages of 18-year-olds in non-higher technical and vocational education are shown in Table 53:[12]

Table 53: Percentages of 18-year-olds in non-higher technical and vocational education, 1970s.

Germany	1979	51.8	Greece	1975	11.3
Switzerland	1976	48.9	Spain	1978	6.9
Yugoslavia	1975	35.4	France	1979	6.7
Denmark	1977	30.3	UK	1976	5.7
Norway	1976	16.0			

In more detail the activities of young people immediately after compulsory schooling were as follows:

Table 54: The experience of young people after compulsory schooling, 1977–80 in percentages

	Full time general education	Full time vocational education	Apprentice-ships	Work or unemployed
West Germany 1980	25	18	50	7
Switzerland 1978–9	20	9	52	19
Great Britain 1977	32	10	14	44

The very low levels of apprenticeship and the excessive numbers going straight into work (or the dole) without prior or accompanying training was a dangerous English peculiarity.

Awareness of this has led to attempts to improve the situation in England notably with the Youth Training Scheme. At the present time the participation of 16 to 18 year olds in education and training is as follows:

Table 55: Comparative percentages of 16- to 18-year-olds in education and training

	Percentages	
West Germany	85	90% of 16-year-olds in Germany and Japan are in work-related training or en route for higher education.[15]
Japan	73	
France	66	
UK	65	including YTS

The initiation of the YTS has narrowed the gap somewhat. Yet even so, our past long-established defects have resulted in the situation that, in comparison with Germany and Japan, Britain's workforce is 'a bunch of thickies' – as Bryan Nicholson (the Chairman of the Manpower Services Commission) vividly puts it;[16] 'The Germans are better educated and trained and have the qualifications to prove it.'[17]

Universities and higher education

What, then, of the universities and higher education? How does Britain compare here? At the beginning of the twentieth century the major industrial countries had rather similar systems of higher education. Most had been created contemporaneously in the previous generation for much the same motives. In England the ancient universities of Oxford and Cambridge were augmented by the civic universities, growing especially between 1870 and 1914. As they grew in size and undertook more degree work, usually external degrees of the University of London, so they emerged into full independently chartered university status. In France the mediaeval University of Paris was complemented by the Grandes Ecoles, like the Polytechnique and the Ecole Normale, in Revolutionary and Napoleonic times. But the modern development was parallel to the English. It was Louis Liard's decrees of 1896–7 which created fourteen new universities from existing institutions in industrial centres like Lyons, Lille, and Bordeaux around the time that the English civic universities were receiving their charters.[18] In America there was a great expansion of colleges from the 1860s. Fifteen universities were created in the United States in the 1860s and the Morrill Act of 1862 gave each state land, the income from which could be devoted to mechanical and agricultural schools. Such colleges of technology, mining, engineering and so forth proliferated so that by the 1900s there were some 500 colleges including about a dozen universities of the first rank.[19] In Germany the traditional twenty-two universities were joined by ten Technical High Schools (the Technische Hochschulen), in effect technological universities, which developed from the 1830s. Both greatly expanded after the Unification.

German university students increased from 14,000 to 61,000 between 1870 and 1914 and those in Technical High Schools from 5,000 to 17,000.[20]

Each system had its distinctive characteristics – the French with the prestigious Grandes Ecoles in Paris, the Americans with a multifarious and democratic spread of colleges and state universities, the Germans with their specialist Technical High Schools as a stream parallel to the universities. Yet the similarities were the more marked. All systems had expanded in the generation before 1914 often creating new limbs – the English civics, the French post-1896 universities, the American state colleges. The motivation that underlay the expansion was common to most. All were industrializing nations conscious of their fierce mutual competition and regarding their education systems as an integral part of their industrial competitiveness. They watched each other's industrial and technological progress at regular international exhibitions while delegations reported on each other's education. All except the French experienced a surging growth of population, which necessitated and justified educational expansion. Ever since Matthew Arnold's report on Prussia in 1868 Britain had been especially influenced by German education, by admiration for the latter's scientific and technical instruction and emphasis on the role of science in society.[21] In the 1890s and 1900s the Education Department's and then the Board of Education's Office of Special Inquiries and Reports further formalized Britain's monitoring of educational developments abroad. By the 1900s there were accordingly strong homogenizing influences at work underlying national characteristics.

We can see this if we compare university attendance between countries at the beginning of the century in Table 56.

There are perceptible differences between France and Germany and Britain but they are small. Only a tiny proportion went to university in any country and the orders of magnitude were much

Table 56: University students in various countries, 1900–14

		Numbers of university students	% of potential university age group
France	1902	30,370[22]	
	1914	42,037[22]	1.65[26]
Germany	1914	77,000[23]	1.47[26]
Britain	1900	20,000[27]	0.8[27]
	1914	26,711[24]	1.20[24]
USA[25]	1910 (completing 4 years)		2.0–4.0 (lower and higher estimates)

the same for the leading European countries with England slightly behind the others. Robert Locke comes to this view: 'There is no need to paint failure in France and Britain too darkly. Since they were industrialized countries with systems of higher technical and scientific education the insufficiencies were marginal at worst.'[28] But already the USA was markedly ahead of Europe in university enrolment and more democratic in its attitudes.

We may now compare Britain and other European countries from the point of view of university students as a percentage of total population.[29]

Table 57: University students as a percentage of population in various countries, 1900-70

	1900	1910	1920	1930	1950	1960	1970
Belgium	0.08	0.11	0.13	0.13	0.24	0.33	0.92
France	0.08	0.11	0.13	0.19	0.33	0.45	1.31
Germany	0.09	0.11	0.19	0.19	0.21	0.43	0.71
Italy	0.08	0.07	0.15	0.11	0.31	0.38	1.04
Sweden	–	0.14	0.12	0.16	0.23	0.50	1.49
Netherlands	0.06	0.07	0.08	0.15	0.31	0.35	0.79
UK	0.05	0.06	0.14	0.14	0.21	0.24	0.46

Britain's slight lag, within very narrow variations, is evident in the pre-1914 period, less consistent in the inter-war years but evident again in the post-Second World War period.

If we take the criterion of percentages of an age group enrolled at university the inter-war data is as follows:

Table 58: Percentages of an age group enrolled at university in various countries, 1920–40

	GB[30]	Germany[31]	France[32]	USA[33] (completing 4 years of college)
1920				2.5–5.0
1921		2.7	2.0	
1924–5	1.5			
1926		1.9		
1930				6.0–7.5
1931		2.7	2.9	
1937–8		1.5		
1938–9	1.7			
1940				*circa* 8

The fairly constant situation in these years and the continued gap between Europe and the USA is evident:

Table 59: University students as a percentage of the relevant age group.[34] 1950–1961

	France	Germany	Holland	Belgium	USA	GB
1950–1	5.4[R]	3.8[R]				
1955						3.4
1958	7.0[S]		8.0[S]	11.0[S]		4.1
1959		7.0[S]				
1960					18.0[R]	4.1
1960–1	9.6[R]	5.4[R]				
1961	11–12[R]					4.1

But the vital issue is the extent to which these low levels of higher education in Britain in the post-1945 years prompted the expansion of the 1960s. It was already evident that in the 1950s Britain was perceptibly behind several European countries with which she ought to have been comparable. Accordingly foreign comparisons played an important part in the decision to expand higher education in Britain in the 1960s.

Robbins' comparison of the percentage of the age group entering full-time courses of British degree level in 1958–9 showed Britain's position:

Table 60: Percentage of an age group in various countries entering full-time courses of British degree level in 1958–9

	% of age group
USA	20 (junior year)
Sweden	10
France	7
USSR	5
Great Britain	4.5
Germany (FR)	4
Netherlands	3

Robbins fairly pointed out that in spite of disparities in intake levels the output of graduates with degrees in science, engineering and agriculture was remarkably uniform – around two per cent in France, Germany and Sweden.[35] The British tradition was one of careful selection and teaching with very low drop-out rates in contrast with democratic first-year intakes followed by rigorous selection and expulsion in the course of the degree in other countries. The British approach is more selective and less wasteful. None the less Robbins considered that there was room for expanding intake levels to nearer, say, those of France.[36]

Michael Kaser took a starker view. Part of Britain's problem was its low economic growth since the war compared with other Western countries. Was there any relationship between higher education levels and economic growth?[37]

Table 61: Levels of university education and economic growth in various countries, 1963

	University students per 1,000 primary school pupils	% growth of GNP
Japan	48	7
Germany	41	11
Italy	35	5
France	28	5
Sweden	17	5
England and Wales	20	2

Such parallel league tables, with England at the bottom, do not necessarily suggest that a country may increase its economic growth rate by increasing its university entrants. Indeed, they may suggest a causality in the other direction – that only countries with fast expanding economies can afford a generous access to higher education. At the time public policy preferred the former inference.

England also seemed to be rather behind in drawing working class students into universities:

Table 62: Working class students as a percentage of total university entrants in various countries, 1950–63

	Germany[38]	France[38]	England[39]
1950		7.0	
1955–6			4.4
1963	6.0	13.0	

Indeed one of the factors influencing Robbins was the awareness of the converse proportion, that only three per cent of manual working class children were at universities in England and Wales in 1961.[40]

Since the expansion of the 1960s Britain's relative position in providing access to higher education has been shown in various 'league table' surveys of proportions attaining this level:

Table 63: Percentages of an age group in higher education in various countries, 1970–82

	1970[41]	1976–81[42]		Graduating 1982[43]	Matriculating 1982[44]
USA	46.5	(1981)	36.9	32.0	61.7
Japan	23.6	(1976)	40.9	34.0	34.2
Canada	33.6	(1977)	24.3		
Sweden	37.6	(1978)	4.5		
Belgium	28.5				
Norway	27.5	(1976)	5.0		
Denmark	26.0	(1977)	4.0		
Italy	24.1			9.0	
Australia	23.5	(1979)	13.3		
France	22.4	(1976)	13.6		29.0
UK	20.6	(1977)	12.4	25.0	30.0
Netherlands	18.3	(1976)	9.3		
Spain	18.1	(1977)	15.0		
Austria	16.0	(1977)	7.9		
Germany	15.8	(1978)	4.3	21.0	21.1
UK ranking	11/15		7/13	3/5	3/5

The figures are not comparable across the columns but their virtue is that they show Britain's comparative position at various points. Britain is not of course in the same league as the leading countries which assume a very high level of participation in higher education – USA, Japan, Canada – nor would we reasonably expect this. Taking the wide range of European countries with one or two advanced 'Western' additions in the first two columns Britain ranks in the bottom half, somewhat below average. There is certainly no evidence here of unusual or massive over-expansion of university students. In spite of the supposed élan of the 1960s and 1970s it appears really very modest compared with most of the rest of Europe. Table 63 highlights two interesting points. British levels of access to higher education have generally been remarkably similar to those of France as three of the surveys show. Thus Robbins' hardly extravagant expectation seems to have come about. On the other hand it would surprise Victorians (and probably many contemporaries) that German participation across all four surveys is consistently lower than the British. The German strength is not so much in a massive output of graduates but in that care for the technical, vocational apprentice training of non–university teenagers which we stressed earlier.

Yet there remain two ways in which British higher education is slightly peculiar – its enrolment of women and its range of subject balance.

Perhaps surprisingly, Britain has one of the lowest populations of women among university entrants of any major country. In the late 1970s just over half of new entrants in USA and Finland were women. Austria, Sweden, Canada, Australia, Italy, Germany, Denmark all have a normal 40–50 per cent. Britain is slightly unusual in that only 39.5 per cent of its new matriculants are women.[45] Only Yugoslavia and the Netherlands have a lower proportion. Robbins had been concerned about these low figures. Only 2.5 per cent of 18-year-old girls went to university in 1962 compared with 5.6 per cent of young men. At that time only a quarter of British university students were women. This rise from a quarter in 1962 to nearly 40 per cent by 1979 is itself remarkable and indeed girls have been major beneficiaries of the university expansion of the 1960s and 1970s. None the less women still make up a smaller proportion of university students in Britain than in almost any other advanced country.

A reason for this may be rooted in another rather surprising characteristic of British higher education, namely its spread of subjects. There is a common misconception that the expansion of the universities from the 1960s has led to an imbalance in favour of the arts and social science subjects. This belief is encouraged by the propaganda surrounding present policies of bringing about a 'shift' of resources from the arts to the sciences partly to counteract this supposed unhealthy imbalance. In fact the reverse is true and this in itself is a British peculiarity. Britain has a markedly lower proportion of students studying arts and a higher proportion studying science and technology than other leading competitors and comparable European countries.[46]

Table 64: The balance of subjects in universities in various countries, 1970s

	University entrants: proportions by subject						
	Arts, Social Sciences, Education		Science		Technology	Medicine	
	M	F	M	F	M	F	M	F
Germany (1978	45.4	61.4	19.8	18.3	20.2	2.4	7.1	6.0
UK (1978)	31.0	50.6	26.8	19.8	22.5	2.4	8.5	9.7
Sweden (1976)	66.4	84.6	12.8	6.4	15.3	2.3	3.9	5.0

In France in 1978 59.3 per cent of all university students were studying arts, social sciences and education, 15.9 per cent were studying science, 4.5 per cent technology and 15 per cent medicine.

The lower proportion of arts students in Britain is consonant with our lower proportion of women in the student body. It is hoped that more girls will be attracted to places in science and technology which should normalize British universities' intake of women students.

Apart from differences in structures and opportunities, there are two other areas where a comparison between Britain and her rivals gives cause for concern. Firstly, there is a disturbing disparity between Britain and others in the performance of schoolchildren in the key subject of mathematics. The mathematical ability of English and Welsh children has declined sharply over the period 1964–81, a drop of nine per cent over thirty-seven tests made.

Moreover, whereas in 1964 England and Wales were third (after Japan and Belgium) out of ten countries tested, by 1981 we had sunk to 22nd out of 24 countries tested.[47] Japan is now well ahead of the rest. This collapse of British mathematical capability does not reflect a biological deterioration of the British brain. More certainly it is linked with the chronic and acute shortage of well qualified mathematics teachers due to their totally inadequate and uncompetitive pay and social position. This is part of the second disparity, the position of schoolteachers. It is clear that the status of schoolteachers varies widely across Europe and Japan. In Germany, Japan and the Netherlands especially teachers are well paid and have a high social status.[48] In Britain by contrast their position is very low. Moreover the perceived status of teachers has a direct effect on the achievement of their pupils. This is a further element in the strength of Germany, Japan and some of our leading European competitors as it is conversely one of our weaknesses.

Comparing our access to education with that of other major countries is nowadays actually rather self-flattering. In truth Britain has been falling down the economic league table for some years since the war. In 1900, when the comparisons of this chapter begin, Britain was the richest country in the world. In 1950 UK living standards were behind only Switzerland and the USA and almost on a par with the latter. In 1960 the UK was still the richest country in Europe, well behind USA but well ahead of Japan. By 1985 Britain had become the poor relation of Western Europe with real income per head between a half and two-thirds that of France and West Germany and behind Italy. Britain is no longer in the first division of economic wealth which includes USA and Germany, nor in the second with France and Japan. We are now down in the third group with Puerto Rico, Yugoslavia and Taiwan.[49] The old industrial and educational rivals of USA, Japan, France, Germany have left us behind. Accordingly our modest standing in many of these comparisons merely befits our revised world position. This is the cause and consequence of our decline – we have lacked the will and now lack the resources to do much about it.

A change in attitudes

Meanwhile we must do the best we can. The arrival of Mr Kenneth Baker at the DES has brought a more pragmatic and realistically imaginative approach, notably in his proposals for the new City Technology Colleges. Yet if things are really to improve in the future we need not only specific measures but a general shift in certain underlying attitudes.

First, we need to return to something like the old 'national efficiency' vision of the Edwardians. They had a firm belief in the role of education as an essential foundation of the strength of science and industry. Moreover they combined this with a frank acceptance of the role of the state. In recent years there has been a revival of Benthamist Utilitarianism – early Victorian Liberal suspicions of the state masquerading as Toryism, without the old Benthamite commitment to state education. The Joseph–Thatcher concern to 'roll back the frontiers of the state' has compromised their custodianship of public education. These are not German or French attitudes to education and science. A more positive acceptance of public education as one of the functions of a modern industrial state would be desirable. So would fewer accusations that education has become too 'dependent' on the 'nanny state'. Most tax payers rightly expect the state to educate their children efficiently as they expect to be defended and to have basic health care provided. There is nothing reprehensible in this and recent by-elections suggest that there may well be a reaction against the yearnings to return to the ideologies of the 1820s which have underlain some politico-intellectual attitudes since 1979.

Second, if we need a more positive attitude to the state private initiatives also need to be fostered. The independent schools are flourishing and providing an excellent service. Policies to abolish them would seem well nigh incredible. Indeed one hopes that private provision will spread in other areas. The independent University of Buckingham is an enterprising and imaginative venture yet its limitation is that its curriculum is chiefly based on the arts and business studies. It has not been able to attract the resources to enable it to develop expensive, 'hard', 'big' science. One would like to see more large scale industry-supported scientific and technical education – a private high-powered University of Technology financed by and subject to ICI, GEC and the rest rather than the state?

Third, and connected with that, we need to be perhaps less reverential about education and less coy about training. It might be argued that since 1918 there has been too much attention paid to education at the expense of vocational training. We have deplored the loss of the Junior Technical School and Trade Continuation School. The 1944 division of academic grammar school passes and also-ran technical and modern 'failures' was equally deplorable for its implied denigration of non-academic subjects. The excessive amount of humanities teaching in polytechnics ('artytechnics') is another manifestation of this bias.

But most important of all there needs to be a more realistic approach by the Government to the teaching profession at all levels. The profession in certain areas is patently inadequate, an inadequacy arising from levels of pay too low to attract the sufficiently able or qualified to perform the tasks expected of them. The anxieties of parents who feel compelled to move their off-spring to independent schools, and the complaints of employers, are consequences of this. This is most obvious in mathematics, the crafts and sciences.[50] But the general quality of all teachers, irrespective of subject, their character and personality is the main bulwark against the 'yobbo' culture which the former DES Minister of State, Christopher Patten, has rightly denounced. Not enough is invested in that bulwark which in some places has manifestly crumbled. We pay the price in other ways – permissive behaviour, soaring crime rates, drunken hooliganism, vandalism and squalor and a prison population (nearly 50,000 in 1987) at a record level. The chronic disparity between high-rated 7–10 per cent 'market forces' private sector pay increases and the low-rated public service settlements barely meeting inflation have helped to create this impasse. The end result may well entail salary dif-ferentials and assessment which should not be resisted. Mathe-matics and other teachers are not Argentinian marauders to be beaten down. They vote with their feet and goodwill, and failure to satisfy them poses greater perils (in the decline of British science, for example) than those other threats to the national honour and well being.[51]

Since 1900 England has widened access to education at all levels.

Its performance has been creditable and in many ways followed the common European experience, driven by the same democratic and economic concerns. This has not been without wrong turnings and culs-de-sac. Among these has certainly been the underemphasis on technical training for non-academic teenagers. It was neglected in the 1920s to save money, after 1944 because of the prestige of the academic grammar school and in the 1960s as the thrust of attention was diverted to 'equality', the comprehensives and university expansion. Also to be deplored was the waste of ability of those excluded from secondary education in the inter-war years. Equally so is the inadequate state of science teaching in the 1980s due to the calculated underpayment of teachers. More controversially some will deplore the consignment as 'failures' of so many to the secondary moderns of the 1950s, others will regret the abolition of the grammar schools from the 1960s. Other aspects of the flow we undoubtedly got right – the Morant reforms of the 1900s, the freedom accorded to the public schools supplemented by assisted places, the great days of the grammar schools from the 1930s to the 1950s as the 'ladder' for talent of modest means, the expansion of higher education in the 1960s in line with demographic need and international experience.

Dr A.L. Rowse, writing of Oxford, reminds us that 'a mere expansion of numbers is nothing to be proud of . . . exceptional achievements are always the work of exceptional men . . . quality is what ultimately counts.'[52] Indeed so. Yet we *should* be proud of the evolution of a more generous education system in which young people no longer face the frustrating struggles which A.L. Rowse himself experienced in search of an education in the early years of the century. There is no harm in struggle for the successful. But there is harm, to the individual and society at large, in the waste of quality and ability that is thwarted and lost in educational systems that deny opportunity and mobility. After all that has been achieved an enigma remains. Is there really much more high ability to be mobilized from the children of the working classes, and what form of education could tap these elusive resources? The next century may have to address this problem more successfully than our own.

Notes

(Details of major sources quoted are also given in the Bibliography)

Preface

1 Alfred Marshall, *Principles of Economics* London, 1890 and 1962, p.176
2 P. H. Wicksteed, *The Common Sense of Political Economy* London, 1935, p.335
3 Harold Silver, ed., *Equal Opportunity in Education* London, 1973

I The Contemporary Crisis

1 *Guardian* 31.12.1985 citing an unpublished survey by Dr Albert Osborn
2 *Daily Telegraph* 25.9.1985 (Henceforth *DT*)
3 *DT* 30.1.1986
4 *The Independent* 9.10.1986 Peter Wilby
5 The Open University, 'The Standards Debate', 3.6.1986
6 J. Marks and M. Pomian-Srzednicki, *Standards in English Schools, Second Report* (National Council for Educational Standards, London, 1985) as reported in *DT* and *The Times* 15.7.1985
7 *DT* 19.6.1985
8 Hansard vol. 76 no. 1342. Written answer 25.3.1985
9 *DT* 5.2.1986
10 *DT* 30.12.1985
11 BBC Radio 4 World at One 10 July 1986
12 *DT* 28.6.1985
13 *DT* 27.6.1986
14 *DT* 22.3.1986
15 *DT* 22.5.1986
16 Irene Fox, *Private Schools and Public Issues* London, 1985, p.144
17 BBC Radio 4 25.5.1985
18 *DT* 17.6.1986
19 *DT* 19.2.1986
20 *DT* 20.3.1985
21 *DT* 21.4.1986
22 *DT* 22.3.1985
23 *DT* 9.7.1986

24 BBC Radio 4 'GCSE: One Examination for All?' 16.1.1986
25 *DT* 3.7.1986
26 *DT* 28.1.86 and 14.2.1986
27 *The Independent* 8.10.86 and 15.10.86
28 *DT* 30.4.1986
29 *DT* 12.10.1985
30 *DT* 27.9.1985 reporting Mr Peter Brooke, the Parliamentary Under-Secretary of State, DES
31 BBC Radio 4 George Walden 2.7.1986
32 *DT* 29.4.1985
33 *DT* 26.1.1985
34 *DT* 29.4.1985
35 Irene Fox, *Private Schools and Public Issues* London, 1985 pp.30, 39 On p.30 Dr Fox lists the occupations of Social Class I.
36 *DT* 2.5.1986 reporting Mr Giles Radice speaking at the Ryedale by-election. Mr Radice is a Wykehamist.
37 *DT* 27.5.1986
38 Swann Report *Education for All* 1985, pp.xviii, pp.62–3
39 *Ibid.* p.71
40 *DT* 17.10.1985 reporting Professor John Eggleston's *The Educational and Vocational Experiences of 15–18-year-old young people of Ethnic Minority Groups* (Warwick University, Coventry, 1985)
41 Swann Report pp.607–8
42 *The Development of Higher Education into the 1990s*, HMSO, 1985 pp.11–13
43 *Guardian* 29.4.1985 referring to Brian Heap's *Degree Course Offers 1986* (Career Consultants, 1985)
44 Gareth Williams, 'Higher Education Deflated' *New Society* 21.11.1974
45 *DT* 17.12.1985
46 *DT* 18.12.1985
47 Tessa Blackstone, 'Access to Higher Education in Britain' in N. Phillipson, *Universities, Society and the Future* Edinburgh, 1983 pp.250–1
48 *DT* 27.9.1985
49 Calculated from *The Development of Higher Education into the 1990s*, HMSO, 1985 p.46 table A8
50 *Ibid.* p.56
51 *Ibid.* p.51
52 AUT Bulletin January 1986 'The Arts Graduate in Society'
53 *DT* 24.6.1986
54 *DT* 7. and 12.11.1985, 2.5.1986
55 *Higher Education* 1985 p.43
56 *DT* 29.8.1986
57 *DT* 15.5.1986

II Policy and Progress from Morant to Butler 1900–1944

1 R. H. Tawney, *Secondary Education for All* 1922, p.35
2 BBC 2 Roger Owen, 'Barriers', *The People's Schools* 25.7.1985
3 B. Seebohm Rowntree, *Poverty, a Study of Town Life* London, 1899, p.397
4 Edmund Rubbra in 'Desert Island Discs', BBC Radio 4, 23.5.1981
5 A. M. Kazamias, *Politics, Society and Secondary Education in England* University of Pennsylvania, 1966 and
Olive Banks, *Parity and Prestige in English Secondary Education* 1955 and 1963 both discuss this whole matter
6 Peter Gordon, *Selection for Secondary Education* 1980
7 Pamela and Harold Silver, *The Education of the Poor* 1974
8 John Burnett, *Destiny Obscure* 1982, pp.88, 99, 305 for these examples
9 Fred Blackburn, *George Tomlinson* 1954, pp.10–13
10 Lynda Grier, *Achievement in Education* 1952
11 Bernard M. Allen, *Sir Robert Morant* London, 1934
12 H. C. Dent, *Secondary Education for All* 1949, p.43
13 *Report of the Departmental Committee on Scholarships and Free Places*, 1920 XV Cmd. 968, p.3
14 Kazamias *op. cit.* p.179
15 Banks *op. cit.* Chaps 2 and 4 for this paragraph
16 Reese Edwards, *The Secondary Technical School* 1960, pp.15–17
17 Brian Simon, *The Politics of Educational Reform 1920–1940* 1974 and Gerald Bernbaum, *Social Change and the Schools* 1967, are both valuable surveys of the inter-war years
18 Michael Sadler, *Continuation Schools* Manchester, 1908
19 D. W. Dean, 'H. A. L. Fisher, Reconstruction and the Development of the 1918 Education Act', *British Journal of Educational Studies*, October 1970
20 1920 XV Cmd.968 *op. cit.* p.36
21 *Ibid.* p.9
22 R. H. Tawney, *op. cit.*
23 Hadow Report *The Education of the Adolescent* 1926
24 Kenneth Lindsay, *Social Progress and Educational Waste* 1926
25 Hadow Report, p.46
26 Spens Report *Secondary Education* 1938, p.88
27 Gillian Sutherland, *Ability, Merit and Measurement* 1984, p.296
28 A. Little and J. Westergaard, 'The Trend of Class Differentials in Educational Opportunity in England and Wales', *British Journal of Sociology*, vol.15, 1964
29 Jean Floud, 'The Educational Experience of the Adult Population of England and Wales as at July 1949' in D. V. Glass, ed. *Social Mobility in Britain* 1954
30 Spens Report, p.310
31 Robert Roberts, *The Classic Slum* 1971, pp.144–5

32 Burnett *op. cit.* p.120 on Edith Hall
33 Ronald Gould, *Chalk Up Memory* 1976, p.9
34 Burnett *op. cit.* pp.128–9; also p.306 for a similar case
35 Lindsay *op. cit.* p.147
36 BBC Radio 4 A woman reminiscing in *In My Young Days.* School, 6.3.1984
37 Helen Forrester, *Two Pence to Cross the Mersey* London, 1974, 1984
38 John Vaizey and John Sheenan, *Resources for Education* 1967, p.27
39 A. M. Carr-Saunders and D. Caradog-Jones, *A Survey of the Social Structure of England and Wales* 1937, pp.119–23
40 J. L. Gray and P. Moshinsky 'Ability and Educational Opportunity in Relation to Parental Occupation' in L. Hogben ed., *Political Arithmetic* 1938, chapter 9
41 Frances Stevens, *The Living Tradition* 1960, p.45, figures for 1938
42 J. L. Gray and P. Moshinsky *op. cit.* chapter 8
43 Spens Report
44 Reese Edwards, *The Secondary Technical School* 1960, p.19
45 W. Alfred Richardson, *The Technical College* 1939, p.54
46 P. H. J. H. Gosden, *Education in the Second World War* 1976
47 *Education after the War* (The Green Book) June 1941
48 Norwood Report on *Curriculum and Examinations in Secondary Schools* 1943, pp.2–3
49 Christopher Hollis, *Eton, a History* London, 1960, p.290
50 T. J. H. Bishop and Rupert Wilkinson, *Winchester and the Public School Elite* 1967, pp.106, 108
51 Christine M. Hereward, 'Parents, Sons and their Careers: A Case Study of a Public School 1930–50' in Geoffrey Walford ed., *British Public Schools, Policy and Practice* 1984, pp.140, 143, fathers' occupations 1884–8
52 J. H. Simpson, *The Future of the Public Schools* Rugby, 1942, cited in Alfred B. Badger, *The Public Schools and the Nation* 1944, p.20
53 A. H. Halsey, *Trends in British Society* 1972. My figures are calculated from the income distribution tables for 1938 on p.91
54 Donald Leinster-Mackay, *The Rise of the English Prep School* 1984
55 W. J. Reader, *Professional Men* London, 1966, appendix 2
56 T. J. H. Bishop and Rupert Wilkinson *op. cit.* 1967, pp.67, 69
57 Christine Hereward *op. cit.*
58 R. H. Tawney, *Equality* 1931, pp.94–5 and appendix I
59 Alfred B. Badger, *The Public Schools and the Nation* 1944, p.21
60 D. C. Coleman, 'Gentlemen and Players', *Economic History Review* February 1973
61 W. L. Guttsman, *The British Political Élite* London, 1963, pp.102–3, 106–7
62 T. C. Worsley, *Barbarians and Philistines* 1940, p.13
63 Spencer Leeson, *The Public Schools Question* 1948, pp.13–16 on the background to Fleming

64 Robbins Report, pp.15–16
65 Michael Sanderson, *The Universities in the Nineteenth Century* London, 1975, pp.242–4
66 Hester Jenkins and D. Caradog-Jones, 'The Social Class of Cambridge Alumni of the Eighteenth and Nineteenth Centuries' *British Journal of Sociology* I, 1950
67 Michael Sanderson, *The Universities and British Industry 1850–1970* London, 1972, pp.98–9
68 Robbins Report pp.15–16
69 A. L. Rowse, *A Cornish Childhood* 1942, 1956, chapter 9 'Getting to Oxford'
70 G. G. Leybourne and K. White, *Education and the Birthrate* 1940, p.255
71 Doreen Whiteley, *The Poor Student and the University* 1933
72 Lord Eustace Percy, *Education at the Crossroads* 1930
73 G. S. M. Ellis, *The Poor Student and the University* 1925, p.55
74 A. Little and J. Westergaard, *op. cit.*
75 Kenneth Lindsay *op. cit.* pp.7, 77
76 D. V. Glass and J. L. Gray, 'Opportunity in the Older Universities' in L. Hogben ed., *Political Arithmetic* 1938
77 Jean Floud, *op. cit.*
78 Major Greenwood, 'The Social Distribution of University Education', *Journal of the Royal Statistical Society* vol. CII Pt. III 1939

III Widening Opportunities: Education for All 1944–1985

 1 J. E. Floud, et al., *Social Class and Educational Opportunity* 1956, p.33
 2 A. H. Halsey, et al., *Origins and Destinations* 1980, p.63
 3 J. W. B. Douglas, *The Home and the School* 1964, p.24. These were grammar, technical, independent and a few comprehensive schools in 1959; most were grammar schools
 4 Frances Stevens, *The Living Tradition* 1960, p.198
 5 I. G. K. Fenwick, *The Comprehensive School* 1976, p.59
 6 J. W. B. Douglas *op. cit.* p.45
 7 Jean Floud and A. H. Halsey, 'Social Class, Intelligence Tests and Selection for Secondary Schools' *British Journal of Sociology* VIII, 1957
 8 J. J. B. Dempster, *Selection for Secondary Education* 1954, pp.40–1
 9 D. V. Skeet, *The Child of Eleven* 1957, pp.31–4
10 P. E. Vernon, ed., *Secondary School Selection* 1957, p.38
11 *Transfer from Primary to Secondary Schools* National Union of Teachers, 1949, pp.84–9
12 Brian Jackson, *Streaming, an Education System in Miniature* 1964, p.20
13 J. W. B. Douglas *op. cit.* p.117
14 Brian Simon, *Intelligence Testing and the Comprehensive School* London, 1953
15 Stephen Wiseman, *Education and Environment* 1964, pp.21, 132
16 J. W. B. Douglas, *All Our Future* London, 1968, p.43

17 Crowther Report, *Fifteen to Eighteen* 1959, p.72
18 P. L. Masters and S. W. Hockey in the *Times Educational Supplement* 17.5.1963
19 *Early Leaving* A Report of the Central Advisory Council for Education 1954, p.5
20 *Ibid.*, p.19
21 J. J. B. Dempster *op. cit.* pp.107–8
22 W. D. Furneaux, *The Chosen Few* 1961, p.145
23 Crowther Report pp. 226–7
24 Frances Stevens *op. cit.* p.20
25 Colin Lacey, *Hightown Grammar* 1970, pp.29–30
26 *Ibid.* p.152
27 Brian Jackson and Dennis Marsden, *Education and the Working Class* 1962
28 R. R. Dale and S. Griffiths, *Downstream, Failure in the Grammar School* 1965, p.19
29 J. W. B. Douglas, *All Our Future* p.48
30 Edward Blishen, *Roaring Boys* 1955, pp.42, 174, and the sequel *This Right Soft Lot* 1969
31 H. C. Dent, *Secondary Modern Schools* 1958, p.143
32 William Taylor, *The Secondary Modern School* 1963, p.170
33 Harold Loukes, *Secondary Modern* 1956, p.89
34 Taylor *op. cit.* p.51
35 Newsom Report *Half Our Future* 1963 pp.197–217
36 Dent *op. cit.* p.14
37 Taylor *op. cit.* p.118
38 Dent *op. cit.* p.152
39 Taylor *op. cit.* p.160
40 Reese Edwards, *The Secondary Technical School* 1960, pp.18–119
41 W. A. Richardson, *The Technical College* 1939, p.41
42 Reese Edwards *op. cit.*
43 Thelma Veness, *School Leavers* 1962, p.162. The study was made in 1956
44 Halsey et al., *op. cit.* p.67
45 David Rubinstein and Brian Simon, *The Evolution of the Comprehensive School* 1973, and
    I. G. K. Fenwick, *The Comprehensive School op. cit.*
46 BBC2 Roger Owen, *The People's Schools* 'Equality' 1.8.1985
47 Robin Pedley, *The Comprehensive School* 1963, 1978
    Tyrell Burgess, *Inside Comprehensive Schools* 1970
48 Susan Crosland, *Tony Crosland* 1982, p.148
49 Leila Berg, *Risinghill* 1968, pp.148–9
50 Rhodes Boyson, *Oversubscribed, the Story of Highbury Grove School* 1974
51 Peter Wedge and Juliet Essen, *Children in Adversity* 1982 dealt with 16-year-olds in 1974; see also Peter Wedge and Hilary Prosser, *Born to Fail?* 1973

52 Julienne Ford, *Social Class and the Comprehensive School* 1969, pp.40, 131
53 Fleming Report *The Public Schools and the General Educational System* 1944, p.23
54 *Ibid*. p.30
55 *The Guinea Pig* a play by Warren Chetham Stroud first produced in London in 1946; the film of 1948 was by John and Roy Boulting who were both ex-pupils of Charterhouse
56 BBC Radio 4 'The Guinea Pigs' 5.7.1984
   But see John Wakeford, *The Cloistered Elite* London, 1969, pp.186–7 for some uncomfortable real-life experiences of 'guinea pigs'
57 James Hilton, *Goodbye Mr Chips* London, 1934, 1978, p.77. The episode is represented as being in 1908
58 George Snow, *The Public School in the New Age* London, 1959, p.17
59 *Ibid*. p.20
60 J. D. R. McConnell, *Eton, How it Works* 1967, p.193
61 Graham Kalton, *The Public Schools* 1966, p.35
62 Ian Weinberg, *The English Public School* 1967, pp.161–3
63 *Ibid*. pp.71–3
64 John Dancy, *The Public Schools and the Future* 1963, p.54
65 Weinberg *op. cit*. p.167
66 Kalton *op. cit*. p.35
67 Wakeford *op. cit*. p.94
68 McConnell *op. cit*. pp.189, 193
69 Mallory Wober, *English Girls' Boarding Schools* 1971, p.277
70 Royston Lambert, *The Hothouse Society* 1968, p.51
71 *The Public Schools Commission* Newsom 1968, vol. I Report, diagram 7 p.59
72 John Wilson, *Public Schools and Private Practice* 1962, p.113
73 John Rae, *The Public School Revolution* 1981
74 A. H. Halsey, *Change in British Society* 1986, p.138, table 6.6
75 Rae *op. cit*. p.160
76 Irene Fox, 'The Demand for a Public School Education' in G. Walford, ed., *British Public Schools, Policy and Practice* 1984
77 G. Whitty and T. Edwards, 'Evaluating Policy Change: the Assisted Places Scheme' in Walford *op. cit*.
78 *DT* 'School Fee Aid Pays Off' 14.12.1984
79 W. D. Furneaux *op. cit*. p. xiii, a study of 14,000 children begun in 1948
80 A. Little and J. Westergaard, 'The Trend of Class Differentials', *British Journal of Sociology* 1964
81 Halsey *et al.*, *op. cit*. p.182
82 Robbins Report, p.16
83 Furneaux *op. cit*. p.44
84 Furneaux *op. cit*. p.40
85 R. N. Morris, *Sixth Form and College Entrance* London, 1969, p.151
86 Crowther Report, pp.226–7

87 *The Age Group Bulge and its Possible Effects on University Policy* Home
    Universities Conference 1955
88 Robbins Report p.260
89 R. R. Dale, *From School to University* 1954, p.26
90 Guy R. Neave, *How They Fared* 1975, pp.50–3
91 Hunter Davies, *The Creighton Report* 1976, p.261
92 Michael Sanderson, *The Universities and British Industry* 1972, chapter
    13, for a fuller discussion
93 Richard Layard *et al. The Impact of Robbins* 1969, p.88
94 Hansard vol. 80 no. 1351 written answer 14.6.85
95 — vol. 73 no. 1337 written answer 19.2.85
96 — vol. 97 no. 1382 oral answer 6.5.86
97 — vol. 62 no. 1323 written answer 29.10.84

IV From the 'ladder' to the 'pool': the concepts behind the system

 1 H. B. Philpott, *London at School* London, 1904, pp.153–4, chapter 10
    'The Educational Ladder'
 2 Bryce Report, *Secondary Education* 1895 vol. I, pp.171, 168
 3 Mr Roby cited in the Bryce Report p.168, for example
 4 Sydney Webb, *London Education* London, 1904, p.26
 5 Eric Ashby and Mary Anderson, *Portrait of Haldane at Work on Education*
    1974, p.112
 6 Webb *op. cit.* p.32
 7 Sydney Webb, *The Education Muddle and the Way Out* 1901 reprinted in
    E. J. T. Brennan, *Education for National Efficiency* 1975, p.104
 8 J. A. Hobson, *The Crisis of Liberalism* London, 1909, p.110 in his
    chapter 'Equality of Opportunity'
 9 Sir Martin Conway 1922 cited in Gillian Sutherland, *Ability, Merit and
    Measurement* 1984, p.287
10 William Temple, *Christianity and Social Order* 1942, 1976 edn. p.37
11 Ross Terrill, *R. H. Tawney and His Times* 1973
12 Lord David Eccles, *Life and Politics* 1967, p.72
13 R. H. Tawney, *Equality* 1931, p.50
14 *Ibid.* p.63
15 Ashby *op. cit.* pp.115, 133
16 Tawney *op. cit.* p.2
17 Lord Eustace Percy, *Some Memories* 1958, p.94, referring to the inter-
    war years
18 *Education after the War* (The Green Book) June 1941 reprinted in Nigel
    Middleton, *A Place for Everyone* London, 1976, p.393
19 Ronald Gould, *Chalk Up Memory* 1976, p.97
20 Mary Warnock, *Schools of Thought* 1977, p.41
21 A. H. Halsey, *Educational Priority* HMSO 1972, vol. 1, p.9 and chapter
    1 generally
22 Anthony Crosland, *Socialism Now* London, 1974, p.15

23 Sir Keith Joseph and Jonathan Sumption, *Equality* London, 1979, especially pp.28–32
24 Viscount Hailsham, *The Conservative Case* 1947, p.166
25 John Rawls, *A Theory of Justice* 1972, pp.101–2
26 Tawney *op. cit.* pp.96ff
27 Anthony Crosland, *The Future of Socialism* 1956, pp.260–5
28 Susan Crosland, *Tony Crosland* 1982, p.149
29 Timothy Raison, *Why Conservative?* 1964, p.104
    A. N. Gilkes, *Independent Education* 1957, on the same lines
30 David Eccles at the Incorporated Association of Assistant Mistresses Conference 1955 cited I. G. K. Fenwick, *The Comprehensive School* 1976, p.107
31 Gould *op. cit.* p.174
32 C. B. Cox and A. E. Dyson, *The Black Papers on Education* 1971, papers by Angus Maude and John Sparrow
33 *Ibid.* S. Stubbs of the Perse School, Cambridge, cited p.189
34 Crosland *op. cit.* p.233
35 Michael Young, *The Rise of Meritocracy* 1958
36 Dennis Potter, *The Glittering Coffin* 1960, p.13
37 Richard Hoggart, *The Uses of Literacy* 1957, chapter 10 'A Note on the Uprooted and the Anxious'
38 Willy Russell, *Educating Rita* 1981, p.12
39 Aldous Huxley, *Brave New World* 1932, p.21
40 T. S. Eliot, *Notes Towards the Definition of Culture* 1948, pp.100–103, also G. H. Bantock 'Equality and Education' in Bryan Wilson, ed., *Education, Equality and Society* 1975 for views sympathetic to Eliot
41 L. S. Hearnshaw, *Cyril Burt, Psychologist* 1979 and Gillian Sutherland, *Ability, Merit and Measurement* 1984
42 Hearnshaw *op. cit.* p.67
43 Robbins Report p.49
44 Newsom Report p.6
45 Stephen Wiseman, *Education and Environment* 1964, p.153
46 Robbins Report pp.49–54 on the 'so called pool of ability'
47 GEC Annual Reports 1984, 1985
48 W. Arthur Lewis, *Theory of Economic Growth* London, 1955, section 4, and *Processes and Problems of Industrialisation in Underdeveloped Countries* United Nations, New York, 1955, were influential statements
49 T. W. Schultz 'Investment in human capital', *American Economic Review* vol. 51 1961
50 H. G. Johnson in *Residual Factors and Economic Growth* OECD, Paris, 1964, pp.219–25

V The Conditions of Progress

1 Geoffrey Searle, *The Quest for National Efficiency* 1971

2 Brian Simon, *Education and the Labour Movement* 1965
  Rodney Barker, *Education and Politics* 1972
  Michael Parkinson, *The Labour Party and the Organisation of Secondary Education* 1970 on these matters
3 *Report of the Departmental Committee on Scholarships and Free Places* 1920 XV Cmd.968 p.11
4 *Oxford and Working Class Education* Oxford, 1908, p.86
5 Geoffrey Sherington, *English Education, Social Change and War* 1981, p.106, citing H. A. L. Fisher
6 Fred Blackburn, *George Tomlinson* 1954, p.194
7 Patrick Cosgrave, *R. A. Butler* London, 1981, pp.7, 91
8 Timothy Raison, *Why Conservative?* 1964, p.100
9 Chris Patten, *The Tory Case* 1983, pp.90, 96
10 Lord Blake and John Patten eds., *The Conservative Opportunity* 1976, 'Education' by Vernon Bogdanor
11 *DT* 22.7.1986 Lord Blake
12 Sherington *op. cit.* p.65 on on the First World War generally
12 *Ibid.* p.137
14 Robert Roberts, *The Classic Slum* 1971, pp.202–3
15 P. H. J. H. Gosden, *Education in the Second World War* 1976, and Angus Calder, *The People's War* London, 1969 on education in the Second World War generally
16 H. C. Dent, *Education in Transition* 1943, p.187
17 Frank W. Mitchell, *Sir Fred Clarke* 1967, pp.111–112; its members included Kenneth Lindsay, Lord Eric James, Sir John Newsom, Lord John Wolfenden, Sir Fred Clarke, W. R. Niblett, Sir Fred Schonell, H. C. Dent, and Lester Smith
18 J. B. Priestley, *They Came to a City*. This was an influential play and film of 1943
19 Beveridge Report *Social Insurance and Allied Services* Cmd.6404 1942 clause 456
20 *Scholarships and Free Places op. cit.* p.12
21 Calculated from: B. R. Mitchell and Phyllis Deane, *Abstract of British Historical Statistics* Cambridge, 1962, tables on pp.396–9, 416, 418, 420–1, 423, 425 on Expenditure 1900–1939; tables on pp.367–8 National Income calculations by C. H. Feinstein 1900–1914 and A. R. Prest 1915–1946; and B. R. Mitchell and H. G. Jones, *Second Abstract of British Historical Statistics* Cambridge, 1971, tables on p.151 on National Income 1946–1965, tables on expenditure pp.160–1, 164, 166, 168, 170
22 Ursula K. Hicks, *British Public Finances* 1958, p.31
23 John Vaizey and John Sheehan, *Resources for Education* 1967, p.139
24 Patten *op. cit.* p.85
25 Sidney Pollard, *The Development of the British Economy 1914–1980* London, 1983, p.408

26 A. T. Peacock and J. Wiseman, *The Growth of Public Expenditure in the United Kingdom* National Bureau of Economic Research, Princeton, 1961, p.92

27 A. H. Halsey ed., *Trends in British Society* 1972, pp.87–8

28 Guy Routh, *Occupation and Pay in Great Britain* 1980, pp.5, 45

29 *Ibid.* pp.13, 17

30 *Ibid.* p.34

31 Sir Michael Clapham, Director (later Deputy Chairman) of ICI at the Conference of the Committee of Vice-Chancellors and the CBI 1965

32 Halsey *Trends op. cit.* pp.83–4

33 Routh *op. cit.* p.120

34 W. G. Runciman, *Relative Deprivation and Social Justice* 1966

35 *Ibid.* p.230

36 *Ibid.* p.235

37 A. H. Halsey, *Change in British Society* 1986, chapter 6 'Mobility and Education', p.125

38 *Ibid.* p.131, table 6.4

VI A Sideways Look: Foreign Comparisons

1 Calculated from statistics on secondary education and population for the countries concerned in Brian Mitchell, *European Historical Statistics 1750–1975* London, 1981, pp.789–803, 29–35

2 Fritz K. Ringer, *Education and Society in Modern Europe* 1979, pp.140, 145, 152

3 A. H. Halsey, *Trends in British Society* 1972, p.163

4 *The Development of Secondary Education* OECD, Paris, 1969 cited in Guy Neave, *How They Fared* 1975, pp.2, 3

5 E. F. Denison, *Why Growth Rates Differ* 1967, pp.106–8

6 *DT* 24.10.1985 citing 'Employer Liaison with Schools' by the Institute of Manpower Studies, Sussex University 1985

7 *DT* 18.4.1985 citing F. Naylor 'Technical Schools, a Tale of Four Countries' 1985, and
BBC1 Panorama 2.6.1986 John Clare

8 *DT* 4.2.1985

9 S. J. Prais and K. Wagner, *Schooling Standards in Britain and Germany: Some Summary Comparisons Bearing on Economic Efficiency* National Institute of Economic and Social Research Discussion Paper no. 60, Industry Series no.14, 1983, pp.1, 42

10 BBC Radio 4 *Woman's Hour* Diana Boesch (an inspector of Swiss schools) 15.7.1985

11 Personal communication from Mr Tim Lambillion-Jameson of the University of East Anglia who visited Japan studying education in Autumn 1984

12 *Policies for Higher Education in the 1980s* OECD, 1983, p.105

13 Sidney Pollard, *The Development of the British Economy 1914–1980* London, 1983, p.408 citing Ian Jones
14 Hansard vol. 71 no. 1333 written answer, Sir Keith Joseph 22.1.1985
15 Lord Young in *DT* 26.1.1985
16 *DT* 21.3.1986
17 *Ibid.*
18 George Weisz, *The Emergence of Modern Universities in France* 1983
19 R. Veysey, *The Emergence of the American University* Chicago, 1969, p.359
20 Charles E. McClelland, *State, Society and University in Germany 1700–1914* Cambridge, 1980, pp.239–241
21 George Haines, *Essays on the German Influence upon English Education and Science 1850–1919* Connecticut 1969 and
    W. H. G. Armytage, *The German Influence on English Education* London, 1969
22 Weisz *op. cit.* p.242
23 McClelland *op. cit.*
24 Michael Sanderson, *The Universities in the Nineteenth Century* 1975, pp.242–4
25 Ringer *op. cit.* p.252
26 Weisz *op. cit.* p.255
27 Robbins Report p.16
28 Robert Locke, *The End of Practical Man* 1984, p.78
29 Calculated from statistics in Brian Mitchell, *European Historical Statistics 1750–1975* London, 1981, pp.29–45, 907–13
30 Robbins Report pp.15–16
31 Ringer *op. cit.* pp.54, 66
32 *Ibid.* p.152
33 *Ibid.* p.252 citing Jencks and Riesman
34 R figures are from Ringer *op. cit.* pp.151, 152, 229, 252, while S figures are from Alfred Sauvy, *Access to Education* The Hague, 1973, p.59. The GB figures are from the Robbins Report p.16. The Ringer figures are entrants as a percentage of that age group. The Sauvy figures are 20-year-olds.
35 Robbins Report p.42
36 *Ibid.* p.44
37 M. C. Kaser, 'Education and Economic Progress; Experience in Industrialised Market Economies' in E. A. G. Robinson and J. Vaizey, *The Economics of Education* London, 1966. Dr Kaser's paper was given in 1963.
38 Ringer *op. cit.* pp.105, 189, 202
39 R. K. Kelsall, *Report on . . . Applications for Admissions to Universities 1955–6* cited Halsey *Trends* p.190
40 Robbins Report p.50
41 *Education, Inequality and Life Chances* vol. 1 OECD, 1975, p.175
42 *Policies for Higher Education in the 1980s* OECD, 1983, p.77

43 Hansard vol. 97 no. 1382 written answer 9.5.1986
44 Hansard vol. 69 no. 1329 written answer 14.12.1984
45 *Policies* OECD 1983, p.219
46 *Policies* OECD, 1983, pp.220–1
47 *DT* 12.7.1986 citing an unpublished survey by the International Association for the Evaluation of Educational Achievement
48 BBC Radio 4 *International Assignment* 'Bottom of the Class' 12.7.1986, Professor Neville Postlethwaite of Hamburg
49 Ian Wrigglesworth in the *Times Higher Educational Supplement* 13.12.1985 and Frances Williams in *DT* 16.9.1985
50 Sir George Porter speaking at the British Association for the Advancement of Science 1986 is but one recent authority to emphasize this: *DT* 2.9.1986
51 *The Independent* 16.10.1986. The Royal Society Report has drawn attention to the sharp decline in the finance, quantity and international reputation of British scientific research and its dangers for our industrial competitive position.
52 A. L. Rowse, *Oxford in the History of the Nation* London, 1975, p.252

Bibliography

Official Reports
(Government, OECD etc. in chronological order)

1895 XLIII Report of the Commissioners on Secondary Education
(Viscount Bryce) C.7862 1895
1920 XV Report of the Departmental Committee on Scholarships and Free
Places Cmd.968 1920
Board of Education Report of the Consultative Committee on the
Education of the Adolescent (Sir Henry Hadow) HMSO 1926
Report of the Consultative Committee on Secondary Education with
Special Reference to Grammar Schools and Technical High Schools (Sir
Will Spens) HMSO 1938
Education After the War (The Green Book) June 1941, reprinted in Nigel
Middleton, *A Place for Everyone* London 1976, pp.391–462
Curriculum and Examinations in Secondary Schools. Report of the
Committee of the Secondary Schools Examination Council (Sir Cyril
Norwood) HMSO 1943
The Public Schools and the General Educational System HMSO 1944
Transfer from Primary to Secondary Schools Report of a Consultative
Committee National Union of Teachers 1949
Early Leaving Report of the Central Advisory Council for Education
England HMSO 1954
Fifteen to Eighteen Report of the Central Advisory Council for Education
(Sir Geoffrey Crowther) HMSO 1959
Ability and Educational Opportunity ed. A. H. Halsey, OECD, Paris 1961
Half Our Future Report of the Central Advisory Council for Education (Sir
John Newsom) HMSO 1963
Higher Education Report of the Committee on Higher Education (Lord
Robbins) Cmd.2154 HMSO 1963
The Public Schools Commission (Sir John Newsom) First Report vol.1
HMSO 1968
Education, Inequality and Life Chances 2 vols. OECD, Paris, 1975
Policies for Higher Education in the 1980s OECD, Paris, 1983

Education for All Report of the Committee of Inquiry into the Education of Children of Ethnic Minority Groups (Lord Swann) Cmd.9453 HMSO 1985

The Development of Higher Education into the 1990s Cmd.9524 HMSO 1985

Books

Abbot, A., *Education for Industry and Commerce in England* Oxford, 1933

Allen, Bernard M., *Sir Robert Morant* London, 1934

Anderson, C. A., Floud, J. and Halsey, A. H., *Education, Economy and Society* New York, 1961, 1965

Archer, R. L., *Secondary Education in the Nineteenth Century* Cambridge, 1928

Ashby, Eric and Anderson, Mary, *Portrait of Haldane at Work on Education* London, 1974

Badger, Alfred B., *The Public Schools and the Nation* London, 1944

Banks, Olive, *Parity and Prestige in English Secondary Education* London, 1955, 1963

Barker, Rodney, *Education and Politics 1900–1951: a study of the Labour Party* Oxford, 1972

Berg, Leila, *Risinghill: Death of a Comprehensive School* London, 1968

Bernbaum, Gerald, *Social Change and the Schools 1918–1944* London, 1967

Bishop, T. J. H. and Wilkinson, R., *Winchester and the Public School Elite* London, 1967

Blackburn, Fred, *George Tomlinson* London, 1954

Blake, Lord and Patten, John, ed. *The Conservative Opportunity* London, 1976

Blishen, Edward, *Roaring Boys* London, 1955

—, *This Right Soft Lot* London, 1969

Boyson, Rhodes, *Oversubscribed: the Story of Highbury Grove School* London, 1974

Brennan, E. J. T. *Education for National Efficiency: the Contribution of Sidney and Beatrice Webb* London, 1975

Burgess, Tyrrell, *Inside Comprehensive Schools* London, 1970

Burnett, John, *Destiny Obscure* London, 1982

Butler, Lord, *The Art of the Possible* London, 1971

Carr-Saunders, A. M. and Caradog-Jones, D., *A Survey of the Social Structure of England and Wales* Oxford, 1937

Clarke, Sir Fred, *Education and Social Change* London, 1940

Cox, C. B. and Dyson, A. E., *The Black Papers on Education* London, 1971

Crosland, Anthony, *The Future of Socialism* London, 1956

Crosland, Susan, *Tony Crosland* London, 1982

Dale, R. R., *From School to University* London, 1954

— and Griffith, S., *Downstream, Failure in the Grammar School* London, 1965

Dancy, John, *The Public Schools and the Future* London, 1963

Davies, Hunter, *The Creighton Report, a Year in the Life of a Comprehensive School* London, 1976

Dempster, J. J. B., *Selection for Secondary Education* London, 1954

Denison, E. F., *Why Growth Rates Differ* Brookings Institution, Washington D.C., 1967

Dent, H. C., *Education in Transition: a Sociological Study of the Impact of War on English Education 1939–1943* London, 1944

—, *Secondary Education for All: Origins and Development in England* London, 1949

—, *Secondary Modern Schools* London, 1958

Douglas, J. W. B., *The Home and the School* London, 1964

—, Ross, J. M., Simpson, H. R., *All Our Future* London, 1968

Eaglesham, E., *From School Board to Local Authority* London, 1956

Eccles, David, *Life and Politics, a Moral Diagnosis* London, 1967

Edwards, Reese, *The Secondary Technical School* London, 1960

Eliot, T. S., *Notes Towards the Definition of Culture* London, 1948

Ellis, G. S. M., *The Poor Student and the University* London, 1925

Fenwick, I. G. K., *The Comprehensive School 1944–1970: The Politics of School Reorganisation* London, 1976

Floud, J. E., Halsey, A. H., Martin, F. M., *Social Class and Educational Opportunity* London, 1956

Ford, Julienne, *Social Class and the Comprehensive School* London, 1969

Fox, Irene, *Private Schools and Public Issues* London, 1985

Furneaux, W. D., *The Chosen Few* Oxford, 1961

Gilkes, A. N., *Independent Education, in Defence of Public Schools* London, 1957

Glass, D. V. ed., *Social Mobility in Britain* London, 1954, reprinted 1963

Gordon, Peter, *Selection for Secondary Education* London, 1980

Gosden, P. H. J. H., *Education in the Second World War: a Study in Policy and Administration* London, 1976

Gould, Sir Ronald, *Chalk Up Memory* Birmingham, 1976

Graves, John, *Policy and Progress in Secondary Education 1902–1942* London 1943, 1949

Grier, Lynda, *Achievement in Education, the Work of Michael Ernest Sadler 1885–1935* London, 1952

Viscount Hailsham, *The Conservative Case* London, 1959

Halsey, A. H., *Trends in British Society since 1900* London, 1972

—, Heath, A. F., Ridge, J. M., *Origins and Destinations, Family, Class and Education in Modern Britain* Oxford, 1980

—, *Change in British Society* Oxford, 1978, 1986

Hattersley, Roy, *A Yorkshire Boyhood* London, 1983

Hearnshaw, L. S., *Cyril Burt, Psychologist* London, 1979

Hicks, Ursula K., *British Public Finances 1880–1952* Oxford, 1958

Hogben, Lancelot, ed., *Political Arithmetic* London, 1938

Hoggart, Richard, *The Uses of Literacy* London, 1957

Huxley, Aldous, *Brave New World* London 1932, 1960

Iremonger, F. A. *William Temple* Oxford, 1948

Jackson, Brian and Marsden, Dennis, *Education and the Working Class* London, 1962, 1966

—, *Streaming, an Education System in Miniature* London, 1964

Kalton, Graham, *The Public Schools* London, 1966

Kazamias, A. M., *Politics, Society and Secondary Education in England* University of Pennsylvania, 1966

Kogan, Maurice, ed., *The Politics of Education* London, 1971

Lacey, Colin, *Hightown Grammar* Manchester, 1970

Lambert, Royston, *The Hothouse Society* London, 1968

Layard, R., King, J., Moser, C., *The Impact of Robbins* London, 1969

Leeson, Spencer, *The Public School Question* London, 1948

Leinster-Mackay, D., *The Rise of the English Prep School* London, 1984

Leybourne, G. G. and White, K., *Education and the Birthrate* London, 1940

Lindsay, Kenneth, *Social Progress and Educational Waste* London, 1926

Locke, Robert K., *The End of the Practical Man: Entrepreneurship and Higher Education in Germany, France and Great Britain 1880–1940* Greenwich Connecticut, 1984

Loukes, Harold, *Secondary Modern* London, 1956

Lowndes, G. A. N., *The Silent Social Revolution* Oxford, 1937, 1955

Maclure, Stuart, *One Hundred Years of London Education 1870–1970* London, 1970

McConnell, J. D. R., *Eton, How it Works* London, 1967

Marsh, D. C., *The Changing Social Structure of England and Wales 1871–1961* London, 1965

Middleton, Nigel, *A Place for Everyone* London, 1976

Mitchell, Frank W., *Sir Fred Clarke* London, 1967

Morris, R. N., *The Sixth Form and College Entrance* London, 1969

Neave, Guy R., *How They Fared* London, 1975

Parkinson, Michael, *The Labour Party and the Organisation of Secondary Education 1918–65* London, 1970

Patten, C., *The Tory Case* London, 1983

Peacock, A. T. and Wiseman, J., *The Growth of Public Expenditure in the United Kingdom* National Bureau of Economic Research, Princeton, 1961

Pedley, Robin, *The Comprehensive School* London, 1963, 1978

Percy, Lord Eustace, *Education at the Crossroads* London, 1930

—, *Some Memories* London, 1958

Potter, Dennis, *The Glittering Coffin* London, 1960

Prais, S. J. and Wagner, K., *Schooling Standards in Britain and Germany: Some Summary Comparisons Bearing on Economic Efficiency* National Institute of Economic and Social Research, Discussion Paper No. 60, Industry Series No. 14, June 1983

Rae, John, *The Public School Revolution: Britain's Independent Schools 1964–79* London, 1981

Raison, Timothy, *Why Conservative?* London, 1964

Rawls, John, *A Theory of Justice* Oxford, 1972

Richardson, W. A., *The Technical College* Oxford, 1939
Ringer, Fritz K., *Education and Society in Modern Europe* Indiana University Press, Bloomington and London, 1979
Roberts, Robert, *The Classic Slum: Salford Life in the First Quarter of the Century* Manchester 1971, London 1973
Routh, Guy, *Occupation and Pay in Great Britain 1906–79* London, 1980
Rubinstein, David and Simon, Brian, *The Evolution of the Comprehensive School 1926–1972* London, 1973
Runciman, W. G. *Relative Deprivation and Social Justice* London, 1966
Russell, Willy, *Educating Rita* London, 1981
Sanderson, Michael, *The Universities and British Industry 1850–1970* London, 1972
Sauvy, Alfred, *Access to Education, New Possibilities* Martinus Nijhoff, The Hague, 1973
Searle, Geoffrey, *The Quest for National Efficiency* Oxford, 1971
Sherington, Geoffrey, *English Education, Social Change and War 1911–1920* Manchester, 1981
Silver, Harold, ed., *Equal Opportunity in Education* London, 1973
—, and Pamela, *The Education of the Poor, the History of a National School 1824–1974* London, 1974
Simon, Brian, *Education and the Labour Movement 1870–1920* London, 1965
—, *Intelligence, Psychology and Education* London, 1971
—, *The Politics of Educational Reform 1920–1940* London, 1974
Skeet, D. V., *The Child of Eleven* London, 1957
Snow, George, *The Public School in the New Age* London, 1959
Stevens, Frances, *The Living Tradition: the Social and Educational Assumptions of the Grammar School* London, 1960
Sutherland, Gillian, *Ability, Merit and Measurement: Mental Testing and English Education 1880–1940* Oxford, 1984
Tawney, R. H., *Secondary Education for All: a Policy for Labour* London, 1922
—, *Equality* (The Halley Stewart Lectures, 1929) London, 1931
Taylor, William, *The Secondary Modern School* London, 1963
Temple, William, *Christianity and Social Order* London, 1942, 1976 edn.
Terrrill, Ross, *R. H. Tawney and His Times* Harvard, 1973
Vaizey, John and Sheenan, John, *Resources for Education: an Economic Study of Education in the United Kingdom 1920–65* London, 1967
Veness, Thelma, *School Leavers* London, 1962
Vernon, P. E., ed., *Secondary School Selection* London, 1957
Wakeford, John, *The Cloistered Elite* London, 1969
Walford, Geoffrey, ed., *British Public Schools: Policy and Practice* London, 1984
Warnock, Mary, *Schools of Thought* London, 1977
Wedge, Peter and Prosser, Hilary, *Born to Fail?* London, 1973
— and Essen, Juliet, *Children in Adversity* London, 1982
Weinberg, Ian, *The English Public Schools* New York, 1967

Weisz, George, *The Emergence of Modern Universities in France 1863–1914* Princeton, 1983
Whiteley, Doreen, *The Poor Student and the University* London, 1933
Wilson, Bryan, ed., *Education, Equality and Society* London, 1975
Wilson, John, *Public Schools and Private Practice* London, 1962
Wiseman, Stephen, *Education and Environment* Manchester, 1964
Wober, Mallory, *English Girls' Boarding Schools* London, 1971
Wolfenden, J. F., *The Public Schools Today: a Study in Boarding School Education* London, 1948
Worsley, T. C., *Barbarians and Philistines: Democracy and the Public School* London, 1940
Young, Michael, *The Rise of the Meritocracy 1870–2033* London, 1958, 1965

Articles

Blackstone, Tessa, 'Access to Higher Education in Britain' in Phillipson, Nicholas, ed., *Universities, Society and the Future* Edinburgh, 1983
Brennan, E. J. T., 'Educational Engineering with the Webbs' *History of Education* June 1972
Dean, D. W. 'The Difficulties of a Labour Educational Policy: the Failure of the Trevelyan Bill 1929–31' *British Journal of Educational Studies* October 1969
—, 'H. A. L. Fisher, Reconstruction and the Development of the 1918 Education Act' *British Journal of Educational Studies* October 1970
—, 'Conservatism and the National Education System 1922–40' *Journal of Contemporary History* vol. 6 no. 2 1971
Floud, Jean and Halsey, A. H., 'English Secondary Schools and the Supply of Labour' *The Yearbook of Education* 1956
—, 'Social Class, Intelligence Tests and Selection for Secondary Schools' *British Journal of Sociology* vol. 8 1957
Glass, D. V. and Gray, J. L., 'Opportunity and the Older Universities' in Hogben, L., *Political Arithmetic* London, 1938
Gray, J. L. and Moshinsky, Pearl, 'Ability and Opportunity in English Education' *Sociological Review* 1935
—, 'Ability and Educational Opportunity in Relation to Parental Occupation' in Hogben, L., *Political Arithmetic* London, 1938
Greenwood, Major, 'The Social Distribution of University Education' *Journal of the Royal Statistical Society* CII pt III 1939
Judges, A. V., 'The Educational Influence of the Webbs' *British Journal of Educational Studies* November 1961
Little, Alan and Westergaard, John, 'The Trend of Class Differentials in Educational Opportunity in England and Wales' *British Journal of Sociology* vol. 15 1964

Index